# Employing People
# in Voluntary Organisations

The National Council for Voluntary Organisations provides professional advisory services to voluntary organisations, protects their interests and promotes new forms of social action.

Other titles in the NCVO Practical Guides series:

# Employing People in Voluntary Organisations

Sheila Kurowska

An NCVO practical guide

Bedford Square Press I NCVO

Published by
BEDFORD SQUARE PRESS of the
National Council for Voluntary Organisations
26 Bedford Square, London WC1B 3HU

ISBN 0 7199 1109 5

First published 1984
Reprinted with corrections 1985

Typeset by D. P. Media Limited, Hitchin, Hertfordshire

Printed and bound in England by
Henry Ling Ltd at the
Dorset Press, Dorchester, Dorset

# Contents

# Practical Documentation

# Introduction

Voluntary organisations now employ many thousands of people and more and more small organisations previously run entirely by voluntary effort are taking on employees for the first time. This is a big step to take and one which places a great deal of responsibility on the members of the voluntary management committee, who will become the legal employers of the staff recruited and will manage and supervise their work.

It is vital that groups who are thinking of employing people ensure that they are fully aware of their legal obligations as employers *before* they appoint staff. Employment legislation is complex and always changing. This brief handbook aims to provide voluntary groups with a simple, practical guide to the main points of the law. It does not aim to be comprehensive. Suggestions for further reading are made at the end of the handbook and groups are recommended to get the publications mentioned, many of which are free.

Problems may well arise in the recruitment or employment of staff which a group is unsure how to handle. In these cirumstances, groups must always seek advice before taking any action. General advice and information on employment law can be obtained from a local law centre or from one of the regional offices of the government's Advisory, Conciliation and Arbitration Service (ACAS).

There are over sixty Acts of Parliament which affect the relationship between employer and employee either directly or indirectly as well as a range of regulations and codes of practice. The rights of employees outlined in this handbook and the corresponding obligations placed on employers are mainly contained in the following legislation:

Employment Protection (Consolidation) Act 1978

Employment Act 1980

Employment Act 1982

Sex Discrimination Act 1975

Equal Pay Act 1970

Equal Pay (Amendment) Regulations 1983

Race Relations Act 1976

Health and Safety at Work Act 1974

Redundancy Payments Act 1965.

The legislation described in the handbook applies to England, Wales and Scotland only. Northern Ireland has its own separate laws.

As well as fulfilling their legal obligations, employers have a wider responsibility to provide decent working conditions for their staff and to follow good employment practice. The handbook assumes throughout that voluntary groups will want to offer their workers the best possible terms and conditions of employment. It therefore describes ways in which groups can improve on basic legal minimum requirements in the areas of sick pay, health and safety, maternity pay, redundancy, etc. It also briefly discusses ways of managing and supporting staff, induction programmes, training and equal opportunities policies.

Voluntary groups rely heavily on the energies and commitment of their paid workers. Providing good working conditions, managing staff effectively and giving them the proper level of support and supervision will ensure that their energies are conserved and enhanced rather than dissipated. This is the best investment that an employer can make.

## Acknowledgements

The author would like to thank Paula Jones, Marie Staunton, Tony White, Richard Peters, and Peter and Gillie Sharp for their help in checking material in this handbook. Thanks to the John Lewis Partnership for a grant towards the cost of producing this guide.

# 1 Before you appoint staff

## Why appoint staff at all?

Before taking the decision to employ staff, consider carefully what it is you want to achieve and whether the appointment of staff is the best way of achieving your objectives. As many developments in the scope of a voluntary group's activities will depend on the availability of staff time, the answer may seem obvious. Yet getting money to pay adequate expenses to volunteers or enough capital to renovate a building for community use may better fulfil the needs identified by the group. Staff are not the answer to every problem and will not be able to achieve miracles overnight. Thinking seriously about priorities for the group and the number of tasks each full-time worker would be able to perform satisfactorily is a good preparation for drawing up reasonable job descriptions and is likely to lead to better work in the long run.

## Are you ready to take on the role of employer?

In becoming an employer, you enter into an unequal relationship with your employees who depend on you for their livelihood. Workers in voluntary organisations face many problems including isolation, heavy responsibilities, lack of promotion prospects, anti-social hours and no overtime pay. It is important that employers realise these problems exist and do their best to minimise them. In small organisations, the management committee must be well enough organised to be able to carry out its legal duties as an employer and to offer a reasonable level of supervision and support to its employees. Think about how the workers will relate to the management committee and appoint one committee member to take responsibility for the employees' work on a day-to-day basis.

It is also a good idea to spend some time considering how the appointment of paid staff will alter relationships within the group.

Will some members of the management committee stop doing so much work when a paid worker is there to do it for them? Will volunteers who have been giving their services to the group for free tend to resent the introduction of paid workers and how will they relate to each other?

## Can you afford to employ people?

The cost of employing people is not limited to their salary and national insurance costs. Employees will travel in the course of their work. They will go to conferences and other events which will cost money. You will want to provide some training for staff for which you have to budget. Expenses may have to be paid for meals out and subsistence. And the cost of stationery, postage and telephone calls is bound to rise significantly. You also need to take into account recruitment costs. Advertising is expensive and the postage costs of sending out job descriptions will be high. It is essential to budget for all these items in any grant application.

## Choosing a salary scale

Make sure the salary you offer is right for the job and apply for that amount in your funding application. If you are unsure what salary is appropriate, ask the local council for voluntary service about similar jobs in local organisations. Ring up other organisations directly and ask what they pay and look in the publications where voluntary agencies usually advertise to compare salary levels.

It is advisable to choose a recognised salary scale for your employees. You will not then need to negotiate cost of living awards each year for just two or three workers. This will be done by the joint negotiating council for the relevant scales at national level. It also has the advantage that your funding body will be familiar with the pay scales your staff are on and it will then be easier to apply for the funds necessary to pay yearly increments and cost of living increases.

Many voluntary sector workers are now paid on the local authority pay scales for administrative, professional, technical and clerical staff (the APTC scales). There are also special scales for youth workers and community centre wardens. If your project has educational aims, it may be appropriate to pay staff on the Burnham scales for lecturers. Details of where to get information about these various scales and the relevant conditions of service attached to them are given in the List of Further Reading at the end of the book.

## Can you offer job security?

Workers in voluntary organisations have very little job security. The minimal protection offered by the law to redundant workers is only available after two years working for the same employer and as voluntary sector workers often have to change jobs to develop their careers, they are usually not protected. Yet many grants are given for fixed terms and when the money runs out, there is frequently no alternative employment to offer to redundant workers. Voluntary groups ought to do all they can to minimise this insecurity. Try to persuade the funding body to make a grant for longer than one year or at least to offer some commitment to refunding if the project goes well.

## Where will staff work

As soon as your funding has been confirmed, think about where your employees are going to work. Most employees will need premises in which to work. Working from home is in many ways impractical and undesirable. It increases the isolation of the worker and arrangements have to be made to pay for telephone costs, heating, lighting, etc. The place staff are to work should be comfortable and accessible. Office workers need at least a desk, a filing cabinet and access to a telephone. Other workers – playleaders, youth workers, etc. – need some private space away from the children or young people with whom they are working. Always think about the special needs of disabled workers when arranging accommodation.

## Discrimination

Before you appoint staff, you should be fully aware of your duty not to discriminate against people on the grounds of their race, their sex, the fact that they are married or the fact that they have a lapsed criminal conviction.

The Race Relations Act 1976 and the Sex Discrimination Act 1975 make it illegal to discriminate against people either directly – by treating them less favourably than you would treat others whose circumstances are not materially difficult, or indirectly – by treating them in a way which looks equal on the surface but is in practice discriminatory. Saying that applicants for a job must be over six feet tall indirectly discriminates against women because most could not meet the requirement. It is also illegal to victimise people by treating them less favourably just because, for instance, they have made a claim of discrimination or helped someone esle to do so. It is also illegal in the employment field to discriminate against married people on the grounds of their marital status.

The Equal Pay Act 1970 and the Equal Pay (Amendment) Regulations 1983 entitle men and women to be paid the same if they do work which is the same or of a broadly similar nature or of equal value in terms of skill, effort and responsibility.

You must ensure that you avoid acting in a discriminatory way when recruiting staff, arranging their pay, terms and conditions, making transfers or giving promotion, providing training or other benefits and services and when dismissing staff. Job advertisements must never normally say or imply that the job is only open to one sex, to single people or to members of one racial group.

You are allowed to discriminate on grounds of race or sex in certain circumstances such as where being a man or woman or being a member of a particular racial group is a genuine occupational qualification for a job. For instance, you could discriminate on grounds of race where the job involves providing one racial group with personal welfare services and this could be done most effectively by a member of that racial group. Similarly, you could discriminate on grounds of sex where the job involves providing personal welfare or educational services that are best provided by men or women or where the establishment provides special care or supervision for people of one sex only. Always seek legal advice before deciding to discriminate on these grounds. In addition, organisations with five or fewer employees are allowed to discriminate on grounds of sex but not of race.

You are allowed to take measures to encourage members of one sex or a particular racial group to apply for jobs where they are underrepresented. You could say in an advertisement, for example, that applications from women or ethnic minorities would be particularly welcome, but do get legal advice before doing this. You are not allowed to discriminate when it comes to selecting the people for these jobs. Applications must all be judged on their merits.

The Rehabilitation of Offenders Act 1974 gives people who were once convicted of a crime the right not to reveal some convictions once a certain amount of time has elapsed. The time varies according to the sentence and the age of the person when convicted. For instance, a period of imprisonment of between six and thirty months becomes 'spent' after ten years. Sentences of longer than thirty months never become spent. People with spent convictions do not need to mention them when they apply for a job. If the employer finds out about the conviction later, she or he is not allowed to dismiss the person or take any other disciplinary action.

There are, however, a number of exceptions to this rule. People applying for a range of jobs including lawyer, accountant, probation officer, health or social worker must disclose their previous convictions. Contact the Home Office to find out if a particular job is exempted from the requirements of the Act.

## Insurance

You must take out adequate insurance to protect yourself from claims for damages from both employees and other people who may be injured through your negligence, your employees' negligence or the negligence of volunteers. There are five main types of insurance to consider.

### Employers' liability insurance

You must by law take out and maintain an insurance policy against claims from employees who are injured or get a disease in the course of working for you. You must be insured for at least £2 million and you must display the certificate of insurance in your office or workspace where everyone can see it. The certificate should be taken down and replaced with a new one when the period of cover runs out.

### Public liability insurance

The compulsory employers' liability insurance only covers you for claims from employees. There will also be other people coming into contact with your staff and coming into your office including the general public and volunteers. Public liability insurance will protect you if these people are injured or their property is lost or damaged through your negligence, your employees' negligence or the negligence of a volunteer. Ask your insurer to make sure the policy includes an indemnity to cover cases where an individual volunteer or member of the management committee is sued for negligence rather than the organisation as a whole.

You should be insured for a minimum of £500,000. If you are running a project under the MSC's youth training scheme, you will be obliged to take out this type of insurance to protect the trainees you are responsible for (see 'MSC funded posts', page 41).

### Wrong advice

If you employ workers (or volunteers) who give advice to the public, you should seriously consider taking out a professional indemnity policy to protect yourself against claims for damages if injury or financial loss results from incorrect advice. Even if advice is given free of charge and statements are honestly made, you could still be liable for damages if reasonable care was not taken in giving the advice. Putting up a disclaimer notice saying that advice is given in good faith but is not necessarily correct usually will not protect you from liability.

### Personal accident and sickness

All the insurance policies mentioned above apply only when someone is at fault and there is a legal liability to pay damages. You may also wish to be able to compensate your employees, committee members and volunteers for any injury or loss of earnings they suffer as the result of a pure accident or an illness. You can take out a personal accident policy which covers accidents which happen during working hours, or one which covers any accident whenever and wherever it happens. A personal accident and sickness policy extends the cover to include periods of illness as well as accidents.

### Employees' fraud or dishonesty

Although this is something most voluntary groups would prefer not to consider, it may be important to cover yourself against loss of funds due to dishonesty. If you do decide to take out a fidelity guarantée policy, be prepared for enquiries to be made into the past history of any employee covered.

To take out any of the above policies, just go along to a local insurance agent, ask for details of the premiums, compare the costs and get a proposal form. When filling in the form, always include all the relevant information no matter how trivial it seems. Anything you leave out or get wrong, even unintentionally, may invalidate the policy.

# 2 Appointing staff

## The job description

A broad outline of the job or jobs to be done will have been submitted with any funding application. If detailed job descriptions were included, these should be revised and finalised. If they were not included, they now need to be drafted. At this point, it is a good idea to appoint a team of management committee members and existing staff to draw up the detailed job descriptions, advertise, shortlist, interview and appoint the new staff.

A job description describes the tasks and responsibilities which make up the job. It should be clear, unambiguous and reasonable in relation to the hours worked and the salary for the job. Remember that it forms part of the employee's conditions of employment and, once accepted, cannot be changed without agreement. The job description should be set out under the following headings:

- Job title
- Main purpose
- Responsible to (which person or committee)
- Responsible for (which other workers)
- Main tasks

If at this stage you find it difficult to define the main purpose, the whole job may need reviewing. It should be possible to define the main purpose in one sentence. For example, the main purpose may be 'to set up and run a welfare rights service for disabled people and to organise and train a group of volunteer advice workers' or 'to initiate and develop child-centred activities at a community centre and to encourage parents to participate in the work of the centre'.

You should then state to whom and for whom the worker is responsible. For example, she or he could be responsible to the management committee and responsible for supervising the work of one community worker and one administrative assistant.

The next thing to do is to list the main tasks which have to be performed in order to achieve the main purpose of the job.

These should be set out in order of importance. For instance, the main tasks to be carried out by the person setting up the welfare rights service could include 'keeping up to date with relevant legislation', 'producing training materials' and 'setting up a library of welfare rights materials'.

If administrative work is to be shared out among the workers rather than being incorporated into one person's job description, this must be taken into account in estimating how many tasks each worker will be able to perform adequately. Typing, filing, dealing with the post and buying stationery do not disappear when shared out between three or four workers. Remember that administrative work is vital for the proper functioning of the organisation, however small. Administrative tasks must be defined and included in job descriptions and a realistic allowance for time spent on each task must be made. You must be absolutely clear about who is responsible for what. For advice on collective working arrangements, ring up local law centres who often operate this sort of system.

It should be possible to type most job descriptions on one side of a sheet of paper.

Once the job description has been drawn up, the selection team must decide what are the minimum qualifications and skills needed to perform the job adequately and what other additional qualities or experience would be desirable. When these have been agreed, they should be written down. This will help you later when you are writing the job advertisement and when you are shortlisting and selecting applicants.

## Information to be sent to applicants

Once the job description is agreed, it forms part of the material to be sent out to job applicants together with a brief outline of the main conditions of appointment, some background information on the project and an application form.

### Conditions of appointment
Applicants need to know the main con-ditions of appointment before applying. Again, one side of a sheet of paper should be adequate to cover the following points:

### Salary and salary scale
Mention the likely starting salary if there is a scale.

### Hours of work
Give the normal hours of work for full-time staff and the pro rata arrangements for part-time staff where necessary.

### Overtime
Say if overtime is necessary and if so, whether it is paid or whether time off in lieu (TOIL) can be taken instead. Do say whether overtime is a regular or occasional part of the job.

### Holidays
Give the number of days allowed per year in addition to bank holidays.

### Pensions
Say whether there is an occupational pension scheme.

### Trade union
Indicate whether staff are encouraged or expected to join an appropriate trade union.

### Relationships with other staff
If more than one worker is being appointed, mention how many there are altogether and how this job fits in with the others. Say whether administrative or secretarial support will be provided.

### Funding
In view of the widespread uncertainty about funding to the voluntary sector, applicants ought to be told the exact arrangements for funding, when funding runs out and whether it is likely to be renewed or not.

### Interview date
Mention the date for interviews if it has been set in advance.

### Description of the project
Job applicants need background information to give them a rounded view of the organisation, its aims and its policies. Established organisations may send annual reports, newsletters and other publications. New groups should provide an account of the history of the project including when it

was set up and why, past achievements, current projects, composition of the management committee, description of the local area, information about any special client groups such as numbers of one-parent families or numbers unemployed, and how and when the decision to appoint staff was taken. A copy of the funding application could also be sent to applicants as could copies of the minutes of recent meetings. Two to four sides of paper should be enough for this information.

## The application form

It is possible just to ask applicants to write in with their life and career history or curriculum vitae (CV) saying why they are interested in the job. However, application forms have a number of advantages. They enable you to ask for the information you want rather than what applicants want to tell you. The information is organised into the same format for all applicants and is therefore easier to compare. And application forms also make it easier to spot gaps and inconsistencies in applications.

The main points to cover in an application form are:
- name, address and telephone numbers at home and work
- date of birth and age
- present and previous employment including latest salary
- education and qualifications
- names, addresses and telephone numbers of two referees, one of whom is the applicant's present or most recent employer
- period of notice required
- applicant's general statement in support of their application.

Leave plenty of space for the applicant's employment history and general statement. A page for each is not too much. Other questions you may wish to ask include:
- Are you registered disabled?
- Do you need a work permit to work in this country?
- Do you hold a current driving licence?

- What is your typing speed in words per minute?
- What languages other than English do you speak?
- Where did you see the advertisement for the job?

Only ask questions which are directly relevant to the job. Questions about marital status and dependants usually will not be necessary. Leave applicants to tell you about any outside interests or hobbies which may be relevant in their general statement saying what they can bring to the job and why they want it. A specimen application form is given overleaf.

When the job description, conditions of appointment, background information and application form have all been prepared, you are ready to advertise.

Make sure that each item to be sent to applicants is as well set out as possible and typed on a decent typewriter. This helps to give them a good impression of the organisation. Print or duplicate at least fifty and possibly a hundred of each item.

## How long will it take?

The time scale for making an appointment from advertising to the time the new employee is in post always takes far longer than you think. The whole process will probably take at least ten weeks.

| | |
|---|---|
| Mon, 1 April: | Advertisement appears |
| Thurs, 21 April: | Closing date for receipt of applications |
| Fri, 22 April: | Shortlisting begins |
| Mon, 25 April: | Shortlisting ends and shortlisted applicants invited to interview Other applicants informed that they have been unsuccessful References requested for shortlisted applicants. Allow fourteen days for replies |
| Mon, 9 May: | Interviews. Successful applicant offered job over the telephone |

# SPECIMEN APPLICATION FORM

## PRIVATE AND CONFIDENTIAL

ABC Project, 200 High Road, Birmingham 021-100 2000

PLEASE COMPLETE IN BLACK INK OR TYPESCRIPT

| | |
|---|---|
| Post Title: | |
| Surname | Initials |
| Address | |
| Tel. No (Home) (Work) | Date of Birth     Age: |

Are you a registered disabled person?

If yes, please give Registration No.

State of Health (please also indicate number of days off for illness in the past two years.

Have you had any serious illness in the last five years?

Name and Addresses of Two Referees
At least one should be a present or most recent employer, or, if appropriate, a tutor. Please indicate in what capacity you know referees.

1.                                      2.

A report from your present employers will be required but we shall not approach them without your permission.
May we approach them now?              YES/NO

| Education | | School | Degrees, Diplomas |
|---|---|---|---|
| FROM | TO | College | Certificates or other |
| | | University | qualifications. Please give dates. |
| | | | |

Employment (including part-time or holiday jobs lasting more than
six weeks) in chronological order.

| Dates | | Name & Address | Position held/ | Reason for |
|---|---|---|---|---|
| FROM | TO | of Employer | Summary of duties | leaving |
| | | | | |
| *PRESENT POST*: | | | | |

Present or most recent salary:

When could you take up appointment?

Any special qualification or supplementary information for the
appointment not covered in previous sections.    (We would welcome
a statement in support of this application.)

Continue overleaf, if necessary.

Where did you see this post advertised?

I confirm that to the best of my knowledge the information given
on this form is true and correct and can be treated as part of
any subsequent Contract of Employment.

Signed: _____ Date: _____

Please return this form to the Personnel Officer at the address
shown on front page, marking the envelope 'Private & Confidential'.

FOR OFFICE USE ONLY

| | |
|---|---|
| Tues, 10 May: | Letter of appointment sent |
| Wed, 11 May: | Applicant hands in notice if employed |
| Mon, 13 June: | New employee starts work |

There are a number of ways of shortening the period between advertising and appointment including setting the date for interviews in advance, telephoning applicants to invite them to interview rather than writing to them, and requesting references after an offer of employment has been made. But it is unlikely that the time scale can be reduced below eight weeks unless the successful applicant is unemployed. It will take even longer than ten weeks if it is difficult to get the selection team together and if rooms for interviews have to be booked.

## The advertisement

The wording of the job advertisement is extremely important. It is desirable not only to attract good applicants but also to deter unsuitable ones because of the time it takes to process their applications and because a rejection is damaging to the applicant's self-respect and this should be avoided if possible. For these reasons, distinguish clearly in the advertisement between essential and desirable experience and qualifications, according to the criteria established when the job description was drawn up.

The advertisement should include:
- the name of the organisation
- the job title
- a brief description of the job and the experience and qualifications essential or desired
- the salary and salary scale
- whether full-time or part-time, permanent or temporary
- the name, address and telephone number of a contact for further information and application forms
- the closing date for applications

- a statement about any equal opportunities policy operated by the group.

If you have a logo, this can usually be incorporated into the advertisement and will help it to stand out but will, of course, cost more.

## Where to advertise

For administrative or secretarial jobs or jobs requiring a knowledge of the local area, advertising in the local press will probably be sufficient. For jobs requiring particular qualifications or a wide range of experience, use the national newspapers and specialist periodicals. Find out also about any mailings or newsletters sent out by other voluntary organisations and include your job advertisement in these if possible.

The main national newspapers and periodicals where voluntary sector jobs are advertised are:

### The Guardian
119 Farringdon Road
London EC1R 3ER
01-278 2332
Monday: Creative, media and marketing (for jobs in the fields of publishing, publicity, community arts and video)
Copy deadline: Friday 11 am
Cost: £30.50 plus VAT per column centimetre
Wednesday: Public appointments (for most other voluntary sector jobs)
Copy deadline: Monday 11 am
Cost: £22.50 plus VAT per column centimetre

### New Society (for social and community work, research and most other voluntary sector jobs)
5 Sherwood Street
London W1V 7RA
01-437 9402
Comes out on Friday
Copy deadline: Tuesday noon
Cost: £16.35 plus VAT per column centimetre (concessionary rates for voluntary organisations and an additional discount to members of NCVO until October 1986)

*Community Care* (for residential and field social workers)
Surrey House
1 Throwley Way
Sutton, Surrey SM1 4QQ
01-643 8040
Comes out on Thursday
Copy deadline: Monday 4 pm
Cost: £16.90 plus VAT per column centimetre

In order to open up opportunities for racially disadvantaged groups, consider advertising in the ethnic minority press. A comprehensive list of ethnic minority newspapers and periodicals is available free from the Commission for Racial Equality. The following weekly papers include job ads:

**Asian Times, African Times, Caribbean Times**
Tower House
139–149 Fonthill Road
London N4 3HF
01-281 1191

All three papers come out on Friday
Copy deadline: Friday of the previous week 5.30 pm
Cost: *Asian* and *African Times* – £4.50 plus VAT per column centimetre; *Caribbean Times* – £4.80 plus VAT per column centimetre

**The Voice**
94 Bow Road
London E3 3AA
01-980 4444
Comes out on Tuesday
Copy deadline: Friday 5 pm
Cost: £5.25 plus VAT per column centimetre

**Handling responses to adverts**
The initial contact between potential job applicants and the voluntary organisation can colour applicants' feelings about the job. Always respond quickly and pleasantly to requests for application forms. Keep a record for future reference of the number of forms sent out, the number returned and the cost of postage.

## Shortlisting

The two days immediately after the closing date for applications should be set aside for shortlisting. Before beginning, the selection team should meet to discuss exactly what sort of person they are looking for and to go over again what qualities and experience they have decided are essential and desirable. This ensures that each member of the team has the same approach and is looking for the same things. They should next decide how many people they want to interview. This should usually be no more than six and no less than three.

The following procedure is suggested for shortlisting:

* Each member looks at all the applications and independently records their own assessment of each one. Applications could be rated as
  * definitely must interview
  * could possibly interview
  * outside chance for interview
  * definitely do not want to interview
* When this has been done, all the applications rated as 'definitely must interview' are pooled together with applications rated as 'could possibly interview' by all or all but one of the team. Discard the remainder.
* If there are still a large number of applications in the pool, repeat the process until you have only twelve or so left.
* Reduce these to the number you want to interview by discussion. Keep the remaining six or so in reserve in case any of the shortlisted applicants cannot come to interview.
* Decide on the order and times you want to interview people (see 'Interview schedule' below) and notify them by letter or a telephone call followed by a letter giving the time, place and how to get there. See the specimen letter overleaf.
* Send letters to all the unsuccessful applicants. See the specimen letter overleaf.

11

## Specimen letter inviting applicant to interview

ABC Project   200 High Road   Birmingham   021-100 2000

Anna Purna

100 The Square

Birmingham                                                15 June 1985

Dear Anna Purna,

Thank you for your application for the post of community worker. I would be pleased if you could come for an interview at 11 am on Friday, 29 June in this office. Buses 100, 200 and 300 all pass close by. Parking space is also available.

Could you please confirm in writing as soon as possible that you will be able to come?

Yours sincerely,


Ben Nevis

---

## Specimen letter to unsuccessful applicants

ABC Project   200 High Road   Birmingham   021-100 2000

1 June 1985

Dear Margherita Peak,

Thank you very much for your application for the post of community worker. I am sorry to have to tell you that you have not on this occasion been selected for interview. We have had a great number of applications and shortlisting has proved very difficult.

Thank you for your interest in the ABC Project and I hope you find a suitable post very soon.

Yours sincerely,


Ben Nevis

---

### References

You may now request references in advance for shortlisted applicants or leave it until after you have made an offer of employment 'subject to satisfactory references'. References can be helpful but should be used with care. They are essential for checking job title and length of service with the last employer but opinions vary about how useful they are in assessing an applicant's suitability for a particular job. As they are an additional source of information in making what is a very difficult decision, on balance it is probably a good idea to get them before the interviews. However, it is perfectly reasonable for applicants to ask that their present employer is not contacted before a job offer is made and this should be respected. Always send a job description when requesting an opinion about an applicant's suitability for the job. Never ask for references without first asking for permission from the applicant (you can ask for permission on the application form).

## Preparing for the interview

### Interview schedule
Allow forty-five minutes to an hour for interviews for professional jobs such as community or advice workers plus fiteen minutes between interviews for making notes. This is far better than getting behind schedule during the interviews and leaving applicants waiting for long periods. Allow half an hour before the first interview for the interview panel to prepare themselves and take another look at the applications and allow at least an hour after the last interview for discussion and selection. It is sometimes a good idea to ask applicants to come in half an hour or so before the formal interview to see the office and talk informally to other staff or committee members.

### Interview panel
There should be no more than six people interviewing and three or four is a far better number. If the selection team is bigger, you need to decide who will be on the panel. Other members of the selection team or committee members or other employees can be given the opportunity to meet applicants informally before or after the interview. Each member of the interview panel should be given a photocopy of each application and the references if appropriate together with a list of applicants and the times they are coming in.

### Planning the interview
In order to conduct a good interview, you need to be well prepared. You should now plan the questions you want to ask applicants. Write down the broad areas you want to cover in each interview and construct one or two questions under each heading. Relate the questions to the qualities you have defined as essential or desirable for the job. You do not have to follow a rigid pattern for all the interviews but it is a good idea to have a basic structure on which to build. Interviewing is demanding and quite stressful. Without adequate preparation, it is possible to forget completely to ask a vital question.

After drawing up a list of general questions, look again at each individual application to see if there are particular areas of experience or qualifications that need exploring. Translate these into specific questions.

When you have decided what you need to cover in the interviews, you should then decide who will deal with which area. Each member of the panel should have a role to play. Divide up the subject areas so that one person, for instance, asks about the applicant's career history, another asks about job knowledge and another about experience of the voluntary sector. Certain members of the panel should also be briefed to respond to questions about the project and about the terms and conditions of employment. You will need an informal chairperson to make introductions, bring people back to the point if they stray too far away, ensure that all areas are covered and bring the interviews to a close.

If possible, interviews should be held in the building where the jobs will be based. Applicants need to see where they would be working if appointed. The room you hold the interviews in should be warm and pleasant. The chairs should be moderately comfortable and arranged in an informal group. Make sure that there will be no telephone or other interruptions during the interview.

Arrange for someone to be available to meet applicants before the interviews, show them where to wait and refund their travelling expenses. Remember to provide access to a lavatory.

## The interview

The way the interview is handled is very important. The applicants will be interviewing you as much as you are interviewing them even if this is not completely apparent at the time. Good applicants will be put off if the interview is badly conducted. If you have prepared for the interview, this should not be a problem.

The most important task in the interview is to make it as informal and natural as possible so that the applicants relax and talk freely. The person chairing the interview should ensure that the conversation flows smoothly with no embarrassing gaps and that it is the applicant who does most of the talking, not the interviewers. A suggested procedure is outlined below:

One member of the team shows the applicant into the room. The chairperson introduces the interviewers and mentions if anybody is a silent observer, such as the representative of a funding body. This should all be done slowly to give the applicant time to settle down and feel at ease.

Another member of the team describes the background to the project. Again, this should be done slowly.

The questioning starts with areas which are not problematic such as asking the applicant to talk about their present job and why they are interested in this job. Never ask questions which can be answered by yes or no.

Follow on with your planned questions. Give signs of encouragement to applicants to go on talking such as nodding or saying 'yes? . . .'.

Do not ask any questions which are not directly relevant to the job. Questions about domestic commitments should only be asked if there is a good reason (if the job entails evening and week-end work, for instance) and should then be asked of all applicants. If such questions are asked without good reason, they could later be taken as evidence of discrimination.

Remember that applicants from ethnic minority groups may not present themselves in the same way as other applicants. Make due allowance for this when assessing their qualifications and experience.

Allow some time at the end for applicants to ask you questions and be sure you have all the necessary information about terms and conditions at your fingertips.

Tell the applicant when you will contact them with a decision.

Another member of the team shows the applicant out.

## Selection

After each interview, all the members of the panel should write down their impressions of the applicant, itemising points in their favour and points against. Otherwise, impressions fade very quickly and by the end of the day, you will probably not be able to remember the first applicant's face.

When all the interviews are over, the members of the panel should compare notes and discuss fully the merits and limitations of each applicant. It will usually then be possible to reject a certain number of applicants and focus the discussion on the remaining few. Sometimes, one applicant will stand out strongly and there will be a large measure of agreement on their suitability. At other times, the issue will not be so clear cut. The decision will be even more difficult if two or three jobs are to be filled and an assessment has to be made of how the applicants for each will work together.

Discussion should continue until a consensus is reached. If agreement proves impossible, a vote will have to be taken. If possible, the panel should agree on a second choice if the first choice turns down the job. In cases where the panel cannot reach an agreement, the job may have to be readvertised. This will mean more time and expense but it is always preferable to appointing the wrong person.

When the decision has been made, someone should telephone the applicant to tell them they have been successful. This should be followed immediately by a letter of appointment stating the main terms and conditions of employment and suggesting a starting date. The letter of appointment is legally binding and should be carefully worded. See the specimen letter below. The successful applicant should be asked to reply in writing accepting the job.

Always record the reasons for the selection of a particular applicant and the rejection of the others. The reasons should relate to the applicants' possession or lack of the qualities you have defined as essential for the job.

Letters should also be sent immediately to all the unsuccessful shortlisted applicants thanking them for their interest in the job and wishing them well in the future. Remember to write to any applicants kept in reserve at the shortlisting stage.

## Specimen letter of appointment

ABC Project  200 High Road  Birmingham

Anna Purna

100 The Square

Birmingham                                                   2 July 1985

Dear Anna Purna,

I am very pleased to be able to offer you the post of community worker following your interview here last Friday. The starting salary for this post is £10,000 per annum. The work is as set out in the job description supplied to you. A written statement of terms and conditions of employment will be given to you when you start work.

I hope very much that you will accept the post. If so, would you please let me have your acceptance in writing and confirm that you will be able to start work on 1 August 1984. Would you also please let me have your P45 and your national insurance number.

If there is anything you wish to discuss, please get in touch with me.

I look forward to seeing you on 1 August.

Yours sincerely,


Ben Nevis

---

### The contract of employment

A contract of employment can exist without anything at all being written down. When you offer someone a job and she or he accepts it by starting work, the contract is made. You may have discussed with the employee some of the main terms and conditions of the contract, such as salary and hours of work, but the contract will not consist of these terms alone. All contracts of employment are affected by a range of express and implied terms arising from common law, employment legislation, collective agreement where there is a recognised trade union, custom, practice and oral or written agreements between employer and employee.

Express terms are those which have

been specifically agreed orally or in writing by the employer and employee. Express terms can be found in the letter of appointment, in the written statement of terms and conditions which you are legally obliged to give to new employees after thirteen weeks in your employment (see chapter 3, 'Keeping Staff') and in any collective agreement reached with a trade union.

Implied terms are those terms which are not spelled out in so many words but which still affect the contract. Over the years, judges have decided that there are a number of implied terms which are automatically part of any contract of employment unless they are expressly excluded. These include the employer's duty to pay wages, to provide a safe system of work and to treat the employee with courtesy and the employee's duty to be ready and willing to work, to obey reasonable instructions and to give honest and faithful service. Terms can also be implied from custom and practice within a particular industry.

The other main source of terms of employment is employment legislation. The rights given to employees by Acts of Parliament such as the right to get equal pay for equal work, not to be dismissed unfairly and not to be discriminated against on grounds of sex or race affect all contracts of employment. These rights are discussed in the appropriate sections of this handbook. What needs to be said here is that in most cases, employers cannot agree terms which override these legal rights. You can improve on them but you cannot reduce them.

**Fixed term contracts**

There are two types of employment contract: open and fixed term. An open contract can be ended by either side giving notice. A fixed term contract is one which is arranged to come to an end after a specified time. A precise date does not have to be given. It is enough if it is set to end when a certain event happens such as the end of a training course or the production of a report. It should also be noted that even if there is provision for notice to be given on either side before the end of the contract, it is still a fixed term contract if it is for a fixed period.

Many voluntary groups faced with a grant for funding for a limited period think that arranging a fixed term contract will be the answer to their problems. This is not the case. Fixed term contracts have a number of disadvantages for employers. The first thing to remember is that employers who fail to renew a fixed term contract when it expires can be sued for unfair dismissal in exactly the same way as if they had actively ended the contract. Employees with fixed term contracts can also claim redundancy pay.

If the fixed term contract is for over one year, employees can agree in writing to forfeit their right to protection from unfair dismissal if the contract is not renewed. If the contract is for two years or more, they can also agree to forfeit their right to redundancy pay. Even so, there is still the problem of what happens if the employer wants to end the contract before the agreed expiry date. If there are no provisions for giving notice and the employer dismisses the employee for anything other than gross misconduct, the organisation could be sued for breach of contract. If there are provisions for giving notice and the employer follows them, the employee could claim unfair dismissal because she or he has only forfeited the right to claim unfair dismissal *at the expiry of the contract*.

These difficulties mean that fixed term contracts are not a good way of dealing with fixed term funding and they should be avoided. It is better to give employees an open contract. If and when funding runs out and dismissal is unavoidable, the grounds for dismissal will be redundancy. It is interesting to note here that the Manpower Services Commission, now a major source of short-term funding for the voluntary sector, has expressly advised its funded bodies to avoid giving fixed term contracts (see 'MSC funded posts', page 40).

**Probationary periods**

If you wish to put new employees on a probationary period to find out if they are suitable for the job, you should be quite clear about how you will use that period to assess their performance. The probationary period should not be too long – between three and six months is probably long enough – and employees must be told they are on probation and what the terms of the probation are. You must supervise staff properly throughout the whole period, continuously review their progress, warn them of any shortcomings and at the end make an honest and reasonable assessment of their capabilities.

When you have made a good appointment, you will want to ensure that you keep your staff. The best way to do this is to provide good management and decent working conditions for staff. This will enable both the workers and the management committee to concentrate on the most important thing: the job to be done. This chapter considers a range of issues which affect the welfare of people at work. In each case, the legal obligations of employers are outlined and distinguished from the requirements of good practice.

### Written statement of terms and conditions of employment

You must by law give all your employees who work sixteen or more hours a week a written statement of the main terms and conditions of their employment within thirteen weeks of their starting work. Employees who work between eight and sixteen hours a week are only entitled to this statement when they have worked for you for five years. The written statement must include the following information:

*Name of employee*

*Job title*

*Name of employer and the date employment began.* If any period of employment with a previous employer counts as part of the employee's continuous period of employment, this should be mentioned. For example, the employee may have been working for a voluntary organisation which set up a new project with a separate management committee which is now their employer. In this case, the previous period of employment could be counted. This is an important point because it affects entitlement to benefits such as redundancy payments.

*The scale or rate of pay* including any information about overtime pay and how it is calculated.

*Intervals of pay.* Whether employees are paid weekly or monthly or over some other period.

*Normal hours of work.* Include obligatory overtime.

*Holiday entitlement* including entitlement to bank holidays. Employees have no statutory rights to holidays, even bank holidays. You should state here the methods of working out entitlement to holiday pay if an employee leaves during the year. Twenty days holiday, for instance, is equal to one and two-thirds days per month worked.

*Sick pay arrangements.* You should mention the statutory sick pay scheme and any additional arrangements (see 'Sick pay', page 28).

*Pensions and pensions schemes.* If you have an occupational pension scheme over and above the state scheme, mention it here (see 'Pensions', page 29).

*Period of notice* the employee must give to you and you to the employee. Under the law, employees working sixteen hours or more a week (and those who have worked between eight and sixteen hours a week for at least five years) must give one week's notice after one month. The employer must give the employee one week's notice after one month's employment; two weeks after two years' employment and one additional week for every year of employment after this up to a maximum of twelve weeks' notice. If the contract is for a fixed term, the date of expiry should be stated here.

If there are no agreed terms and conditions under any of these headings, you must say so.

The written statement must also include an additional note about the disciplinary and grievance procedures you operate. It must set out any disciplinary rules and say who the employee should get in touch with if she or he has a grievance or is dissatisfied with a disciplinary decision (see 'Disciplinary and grievance procedures', page 31).

If you have an occupational pension scheme and have contracted out of the state scheme, you must state that you have a contracted out certificate.

If any change is agreed in the terms and conditions, you must inform all your employees within one month of the change.

There are a number of subjects you are not obliged to cover in the written statement including maternity and paternity leave and pay, compassionate leave and time off work for public duties and trade union activities. It is good practice, however, to incorporate details of agreed terms and conditions in these areas into your written statement. Each subject is dealt with separately in the remaining part of this chapter and a specimen written statement covering all the relevant areas is given in Appendix 2.

## Induction

Induction means helping a new employee to settle down into the job as quickly as possible and to get to know the people, the organisation and the surroundings. This would all happen anyway even if you made no formal arrangements for induction, but it is good employment practice to plan an induction programme. It is very important not to leave employees in an isolated position at the beginning of a job not really knowing what their priorities should be. This is especially important in the chaotic and unformed atmosphere of a new project. Allowing time for induction should be seen as an investment in the future of the project.

Even the smallest organisation can arrange a good induction programme. Think carefully about what the employee needs to know in order to do the job effectively. She or he will need to know about the priorities of the project as a whole and any problems it faces; how her or his job fits in; and how the project relates to the outside world. The induction programme could therefore include:
• informal briefing sessions from key people within the project
• meetings with key people in the local area
• visits to other relevant local voluntary organisations
• attendance at meetings of other voluntary organisations
• visits to relevant local authority departments

- attendance at local authority council meetings and relevant sub-committee meetings
- time for reading through background material such as reports, minutes, etc.

Do not forget that someone should be there to show the employee round on her or his first day at work. Induction should not be too intensive. One or two briefing sessions and one or two visits spread over two months or so should leave the employee enough time to get to grips with the job as well. At the end, discuss with the employee how the induction programme went and whether any areas of work are still unclear.

## Managing and supporting staff

The arrangements you make for managing and supporting staff are extremely important. Management and support go hand in hand. You must, for your own sake and for the sake of the funders of the project, supervise your employees to ensure that they are performing their work adequately. Employees will not, however, be able to function effectively unless they receive support and encouragement and have regular opportunities to review their work and discuss any problems that arise. In order to supervise staff effectively, you must:
- ensure that the aims of the organisation are clear
- know what the employee is meant to be doing
- know what the employee is actually doing.

Setting out the aims of the organisation as a whole provides a context and framework for assessing the work of each employee. The organisation's objectives, both long term and short term, should be reviewed regularly and progress should be measured. It is also essential that both the management committee and the employee understand what the employee is supposed to be doing. Each worker ought to have a clear job description which is reviewed regularly to check that it is realistic.

In a small voluntary organisation, employees will usually be responsible directly to the management committee for their work and will be required to give written and oral reports at management committee meetings. A brief report once a month plus a more detailed report once a quarter is probably enough. Employees ought to be encouraged to assess their work, not merely to describe it.

In order to find out what the employee is doing and what she or he feels about the job, you will need more than formal reports to management committee meetings. At the beginning of the handbook, it was suggested that one member of the management committee ought to take responsibility for an employee's work on a day-to-day basis. If you make such an arrangement, the committee member will be able not only to manage the employee but also to offer support in an informal way. Without this type of support, it is easy for workers, particularly in a very small project, to become isolated and disillusioned with the job. The committee member should preferably have some knowledge and experience of the work the employee is doing. She or he must also be sensitive to the needs of the employee and not interfere unduly in the employee's work.

Another way of providing management and support for an employee is to involve an outside person who has some special knowledge of the employee's field of work. Employees should also be encouraged to join mutual support groups composed of workers in the same or a similar field.

Finally, remember that members of the management committee might need to undertake some training in management techniques if they are to manage staff effectively. The Management Development Unit at the National Council for Voluntary Organisations can provide information and advice on management training for voluntary groups.

## Health and safety

Health and safety issues are frequently ignored in the voluntary sector. Yet there are many health hazards, both physical and psychological, which may affect employees working long hours in isolated jobs often in poor working conditions. The rapid introduction into offices of microprocessors and visual display units is another reason for taking health and safety more seriously as is the recent rise in the number of employment projects and workshops run by voluntary groups where the safety of processes, products and procedures is of vital importance.

As an employer, you have a legal duty under the Health and Safety at Work Act 1974 to make sure that your employees have a healthy and safe working environment. In particular, you must:

- provide a safe place of work and safe access to it
- provide a safe system of work and safe equipment
- use, store and transport articles and substances in a safe and healthy way
- supervise your employees properly and provide them with information and training on health and safety.

You are not allowed to charge employees for anything done to protect their health and safety. The Offices, Shops and Railway Premises Act 1963 also places a duty on you to provide a safe, clean working environment for staff. To fulfil the requirements of both Acts, you should carry out a thorough survey of possible health hazards at work. Some of the questions you should ask are:

- Is the workplace adequately ventilated, heated and lit?
- Are there adequate means of escape in case of fire?
- Is there a first aid box?
- Is the workplace reasonably clean and tidy?
- Is electrical equipment regularly checked and maintained?
- Are any chemicals used, e.g. in photocopiers, and are these safely stored and handled?
- Are you following good practice in relation to the use of visual display units, i.e. checking for glare and reflection, surrounding light levels, rest breaks, etc.?

- Are all staff aware of health hazards and how to deal with them?

You must keep an accident book in which you record the date, place and circumstances of any accident which results in an employee being incapacitated for work for three days or more.

If you have five or more staff, you must also prepare a written statement outlining your policy on health and safety and the organisation and arrangements for carrying it out. The statement should include the following information:

- a general statement of your intention to provide safe working conditions
- the name of the director, secretary or manager responsible for ensuring that the policy is implemented
- the names of any other key individuals responsible for health and safety and what their responsibilities are
- a description of any arrangements for joint consultation with a recognised trade union and the names of any safety representatives appointed by the union
- details of training in health and safety to be undertaken by staff
- a list of the main health hazards identified in your survey of the working arrangements and workplace
- the procedure for recording accidents at work.

It is good employment practice to prepare a written statement on health and safety whether you are legally obliged to or not.

If you have recognised your employees' trade union, then the union is entitled to appoint safety representatives who will have powers to investigate health hazards, inspect the workplace and get information from you about safety matters. They are entitled to paid time off work to carry out these duties and to undertake training (see 'Time off work', page 26). If two safety representatives request it, you must set up a joint safety committee.

In addition to your specific duties towards employees, you are also obliged to consider people other than employees who may be affected by the way you run your organisation and to ensure that you do not endanger their health and safety. These people include the self-employed, employees of other contractors who are working on your premises and the general public. Trainees on the youth training scheme are also included in this group of people (see 'MSC funded posts', page 40).

## Maternity rights

A pregnant employee has the following legal rights:
- the right not to be reasonably refused to time off with pay for antenatal care
- the right not to be dismissed solely or mainly because of pregnancy
- the right to six weeks' maternity pay
- the right to return to her job provided she returns within twenty-nine weeks of the birth of her baby.

All these rights, except for the first, depend on how long the employee has worked for you, how many hours she works and the number of other staff employed.

### Time off for antenatal care

All pregnant employees have a right to paid time off for antenatal care. You are entitled, except in the case of the first request for time off, to ask the employee to show you a medical certificate stating she is pregnant and/or a document showing that an appointment for antenatal care has been made.

### Right not to be dismissed

Only an employee who has worked full time (sixteen or more hours a week) for at least one year (two years in the case of employees starting work on or after 1 June 1985) or part time (between eight and sixteen hours a week) for at least five years is entitled to claim unfair dismissal. In addition, employees in organisations with twenty or fewer employees can only claim unfair dismissal when they have worked there for at least two years. Dismissal on grounds of pregnancy or a reason related to pregnancy is considered automatically unfair unless the woman's condition makes it impossible for her to do her job adequately or it would be against the law for

her to do the job while pregnant. In such cases, you must offer the woman an alternative job if one is available. Employees who are dismissed for either of these reasons do not lose the right to maternity pay or the right to return to their job after maternity absence.

### Right to maternity pay

An employee who works full time (sixteen or more hours a week) and has worked for you for at least two years, or who works part time (between eight and sixteen hours a week) and has worked for you for at least five years at the start of the eleventh week before the week she expects to give birth is entitled to maternity pay. She must tell you in writing at least twenty-one days before she stops work or as soon as reasonably practicable that she will be stopping work because of her pregnancy.

You must pay maternity pay for the first six weeks of absence starting at or after the beginning of the eleventh week before the week she is having the baby. Maternity pay is nine-tenths of normal pay less the amount of national insurance maternity allowance whether or not the employee actually gets this allowance. Deductions for tax and national insurance should be made in the same way as for normal pay. You may pay maternity pay in a lump sum if you wish.

### Getting a rebate from the Maternity Pay Fund

You can claim back the full amount of maternity pay you have paid to an employee plus the amount of the employer's share of national insurance contributions. To do this, get the address of the nearest redundancy payments office from a local jobcentre or unemployment benefit office and ask for forms MPI and MPI(R). You should claim the rebate no later than six months after you have made the last maternity payment.

### Right to return to work

An employee who fulfils all the conditions described above for entitlement to maternity pay, and in addition tells you in writing twenty-one days before she stops work that she wants to return to her old job, has the right to return. She must return not later than twenty-nine weeks after the week in which she had her baby. If she is ill, she is entitled, on production of a medical certificate, to put off her return for a further four weeks and you may also ask her to put off her date of return for up to four weeks provided you give a reason.

While she is away from work, you are entitled to ask her in writing whether she still intends to return. You must not do this until seven weeks after the week she was expected to have the baby and you must explain that she will lose the right to return to work if she does not reply in writing to your letter within fourteen days of getting it or as soon as is reasonably practicable afterwards. In addition, she must write again to you at least twenty-one days before she is due to return to work telling you the date of her return.

If you fail to allow an employee to return to her job after pregnancy (or to offer her a suitable alternative job if it is impracticable to give her back her old job), you may face a claim of unfair dismissal. This is discussed fully below in 'Fair and unfair dismissal'. However, if you employ five or fewer people, you are exempted from these obligations and do not have to allow a woman to return to work after confinement if it is impracticable to do so. You have to be able to justify your reasons in case your employee takes the matter to an industrial tribunal.

### Improving on the basic rights

A good employer may improve on these basic rights in a number of ways. Many voluntary organisations grant maternity leave and pay after one year's employment rather than two. Many also provide for a period of six weeks or more on full pay followed by six weeks or more on half pay and a further six weeks on half pay which employees are asked not to take unless they intend to return to work. You ought to try to match these terms.

### Temporary maternity replacements

If you take on an employee to fill in for a woman away on maternity leave, you should warn her or him that the job is temporary.

Provided this is done, you may dismiss the person when the woman returns to work and she or he will not be able to claim unfair dismissal unless alternative work is available. However, most such employees will not have worked the full year which is needed before a claim of unfair dismissal can be made.

### Paternity rights

Fathers and prospective fathers have no paternity rights under the law. However, good employers recognise the need for some provision to enable men to help their partners around the time their children are born. Some voluntary organisations allow ten or more days' paid leave to fathers to be taken within three months either side of the birth.

### Equal opportunities

The duties placed upon employers by anti-discrimination legislation and the requirement to employ some disabled workers in certain circumstances are described elsewhere in this handbook. However, these duties are minimal and there are also some forms of discrimination which are not specifically outlawed including discrimination against homosexuals, discrimination on religious grounds and discrimination against single people.

Many voluntary organisations wishing to set the pace in good employment practice have therefore committed themselves to developing and maintaining a policy to promote equal opportunities at work regardless of workers' sex, race, marital status, sexual orientation or religion. It is not enough for such a policy to be adopted, written down and then largely ignored. If the policy is to be effective, it must be applied to all the activities of the voluntary group and be regularly reviewed.

Some of the ways in which an equal opportunities policy could be implemented and monitored include the following:

- mentioning in all job advertisements that an equal opportunities policy is operated
- advertising jobs in the ethnic minority press
- stating in advertisements that applications from certain ethnic minority groups and/or from women are welcomed
- looking at all jobs to see whether job-sharing would be possible
- providing child-care facilities or joining with other local employers to provide them
- improving on the legal minimum requirements for maternity leave and pay
- granting ethnic minority employees additional time off for religious holidays
- granting paternity leave and pay
- continually monitoring the proportion of women and ethnic minorities in lower-status jobs
- arranging training for staff such as race awareness or industrial language training
- forging links with local ethnic minority groups
- sending details of jobs to the disablement resettlement officer and local groups in contact with disabled people
- ensuring that offices are accessible to disabled people and finding out about aids and adaptations which may help disabled people to take up a job
- ensuring that all employees are aware of the aims and operation of the equal opportunities policy adopted.

Codes of practice on equal opportunities policies in employment have been issued by both the Equal Opportunities Commission and the Commission for Racial Equality (see 'Further reading').

## Training

Many voluntary groups discount the provision of training for staff on grounds of cost. Yet paid workers are one of the major resources of a voluntary organisation and in-service training is vitally necessary to enable them to develop their knowledge and experience and thus perform their job better. A budget for training, however small, should therefore always be included in a grant application.

A small voluntary group cannot provide a high level of training from within its own ranks. It must therefore use outside organisations to get the training that its staff need. When money is tight, you will be faced with some difficult decisions about what training can be made available to staff, but this should not be allowed to disguise the fact that training is needed. Where the costs of attending a course cannot be met, consideration should at least be given to allowing employees time off if they are prepared to pay for the training themselves.

There are a number of ways of arranging free or very cheap training for staff. You should find out about any relevant internal training courses run by the local authority and try to get permission for your employees to attend without payment. Local further education and adult education colleges often run day or evening classes on topics relevant to voluntary groups such as housing and welfare law, fund raising and publicity. These courses often cost very little.

Staff should be encouraged to attend seminars and conferences relevant to their field of work. The costs of attendance at events such as these will be much less than those for extended courses of study. Employees should also be given time to attend formal or informal groupings of workers in similar fields of work set up to provide mutual support as this can be a valuable form of training.

## Time off work

Employees have a legal right to a reasonable amount of time off work with or without pay in the following circumstances:

### Time off for public duties
Employees who work full time (sixteen hours or more a week) or have worked part time (between eight and sixteen hours a week) for at least five years for the same

employer are entitled to take reasonable time off to perform public duties. The provisions apply to JPs, local councillors and members of statutory tribunals, health authorities, governing bodies of maintained schools or colleges and water authorities. You are not obliged to pay for time off for public duties.

## Time off for trade union duties and activities

Employees who work full time (sixteen hours or more a week) or have worked part time (between eight and sixteen hours a week) for at least five years are entitled to take reasonable time off for trade union duties and activities.

You must allow time off with pay to any official of a trade union which you as an employer have recognised for collective bargaining purposes. Union officials are entitled to reasonable time off to carry out duties which are concerned with industrial relations between the employer and employees and to take relevant training courses which have been approved by the official's own union or by the TUC.

You must also allow time off without pay to members of the trade union you have recognised to enable them to take part in union activities and to act as a representative of the union except where the activities consist of industrial action.

The Advisory, Conciliation and Arbitration Service (ACAS) publishes a code of practice on time off for trade union activities which outlines what should be taken into consideration when arranging time off for employees.

## Time off for safety representatives

The Health and Safety at Work Act 1974 gives safety representatives appointed by a trade union which is recognised by the employer the right to time off with pay to carry out their duties and to take training courses in health and safety which are approved by their union or by the TUC.

The Health and Safety Commission issues regulations on safety representatives and safety committees which give guidance on what amount of time off is reasonable.

## Time off to look for work for redundant employees

Employees facing redundancy are entitled to reasonable time off with pay to look for other work or to arrange a training course which will help them to get another job. They must, however, have worked full time (sixteen or more hours a week) for at least two years or part time (between eight and sixteen hours a week) for five years for the same employer.

## Time off for antenatal care

Pregnant employees have a right to take time off with pay for antenatal care provided they have an appointment.

## Compassionate leave

Apart from the legal rights mentioned above, you ought to make some arrangements for staff to be granted compassionate leave in cases of bereavement or severe illness of a close friend or relative. It is best to leave the circumstances in which leave will be granted quite open to take account of unforeseen events.

## Paying staff: PAYE and national insurance

As an employer, you are responsible for paying your staff, providing them with payslips, making the correct deductions from their wages for tax and national insurance and paying these amounts, together with the employer's national insurance contributions, to the Inland Revenue each month. The work is fairly simple and straightforward but accuracy is essential and proper and complete records must be kept. You will save yourself a lot of time if you can arrange for the local authority to pay your staff for you or if one of your employees takes on the work.

## Itemised payslips

Every employee is entitled to get a detailed payslip each time they are paid. The payslip should include the following information:
- the gross amount of wages or salary
- the amounts of any variable deductions such as tax and national insurance

- the amounts of any fixed deductions such as trade union subscriptions
- the net amount of wages or salary payable.

You can buy preprinted payslips from any office stationery shop. Remember that manual workers have the right to be paid in cash.

## PAYE

Pay As You Earn or PAYE is the method used for deducting tax on a regular weekly or monthly basis from the wages or salaries of all employees. PAYE operates in parallel with the system for making national insurance contributions and for recovering the amount of any statutory sick pay paid to employees. National insurance is dealt with below and statutory sick pay is covered on page 28.

As soon as you know you will be employing staff, ring up a local office of the Inland Revenue giving the address of your office or workplace. They will tell you which tax office covers your area. A tax reference number will then be allocated to you and all the necessary forms and instructions for operating PAYE will be sent to you including the Employer's guide to PAYE (P7) and the 'blue card' (P8).

### New employees

When you take on a new employee, she or he will normally bring a form P45 from her or his previous employer. This gives the employee's tax code and national insurance number and the amount of pay and tax paid to date. You keep part 2 of the form and send part 3 off to the tax office.

If the employee does not produce a form P45 and she or he is going to be working for you for longer than a week, you should fill in a form P46 and send it off to the tax office to obtain the correct tax code. In the meantime, you should use the emergency tax code. You should start a deduction working sheet (P11 (new)) for each new employee.

### Calculating PAYE

When you know the correct tax code for the new employee, calculating the amount of tax due is straightforward. You will need copies of the free pay tables and the taxable

pay tables issued by the tax office Copies of the tax tables should be made available to employees who wish to check the deductions made from their pay.

At the end of each financial year, you must give each of your employees a form P60 which states their earnings and the amount of tax paid during the year. When an employee leaves, you must prepare a form P45 containing the information described above. Send part 1 to the tax office and give parts 2 and 3 to the employee to give to her or his new employer.

### Temporary and casual staff

You must prepare a deductions working sheet and deduct tax if the employee earns more than the tax threshold. The current rates are shown on the 'blue card'. Where the employee earns less than the tax threshold, you should keep a record of her or his name and address and the amount of money paid.

### National insurance

Class I national insurance contributions have to be paid for all employees earning over the national insurance lower earnings limit which is set by government each year and is slightly less than the tax threshold (£35.50 per week in April 1985). Contributions are due from employees and from employers on behalf of employees. You will generally pay contributions at the 'not-contracted-out' rate unless you have an approved pensions scheme which allows you to pay contributions at the 'contracted-out' rate. Basically, 'not-contracted-out' means that you pay the full amount of contributions which entitle your employees to both the basic and the additional state pension. 'Contracted-out' means you pay a reduced rate and your employees receive the basic state pension only and get an occupational pension instead of the additional state pension (see 'Pensions', page 29).

The not-contracted-out contribution tables are issued automatically to new employers by the tax office. To calculate the contribution due, look up the employee's gross pay for the week or month in the appropriate table. Enter the amounts on the employee's deductions working sheet (P11 (new)), and deduct the employee's contribution from her or his salary.

Some married women are entitled to pay reduced contributions and employees over pension age do not have to pay contributions although you are still required to pay the employer's contribution for these employees. In both cases, the employee should give you a certificate saying they pay reduced contributions or no contributions.

## Paying tax and national insurance to the Inland Revenue

You should pay the total amount of tax and national insurance contributions due for all your employees to the Inland Revenue within fourteen days of the end of the tax month using payslip P30(Z).

## Sick pay

You will need to make some arrangements for paying your staff when they are too ill to work and for them to notify you of their illness. The legal minimum requirement is that you operate the government's statutory sick pay scheme.

### Statutory sick pay

Most employees who earn over the national insurance lower earnings limit (£35.50 per week in April 1985) are entitled to statutory sick pay (SSP). The exceptions include workers taken on for a fixed period of three months or less, pregnant workers who are off sick at any time from the start of the eleventh week before the birth to the end of the sixth week after, and anyone who has received a state benefit such as sickness benefit or maternity allowance within the last fifty-seven days.

SSP is paid to employees direct by the employer (who then claims it back from the Inland Revenue) and is only payable for eight weeks in any one tax year. There are three rates of SSP – higher, middle and lower – which are related to the employee's normal gross earnings. SSP payments are treated in exactly the same way as normal

pay and both tax and national insurance should be deducted.

Before you can operate the scheme, you need to decide which days will count as qualifying days for SSP. You should agree the qualifying days in consultation with your staff and they will usually be the normal working days, i.e. Monday to Friday or Monday to Saturday.

Employees are entitled to SSP when
• they have been off sick for four days or more
• all the four days are qualifying days.

You should consult the guidelines on payment of SSP produced by the DHSS, these should normally be provided with your tax tables.

SSP should be paid as part of the employee's normal salary on the appropriate payday. You must keep records of both the amounts paid and the number of days of sickness for each employee. A record sheet (SSP2) is available from the DHSS. You also record SSP on your PAYE deductions working sheet (see 'Paying staff', page 26).

Fourteen days before an employee's entitlement to SSP runs out, you must send her or him a form SSP1(T) saying that SSP will run out soon and advising the employee that she or he may be able to claim state sickness benefit.

### Recovering statutory sick pay

To recover any SSP you have had to pay in a particular month, simply deduct the gross amount of SSP from the national insurance contributions you are due to pay before you send in your cheque for tax and national insurance to the Inland Revenue (see 'Paying staff', page 26).

### Notification of illness and self-certification

You must make clear to your staff how you wish them to notify you that they are ill whether by telephone or letter or both. You must also decide what form of certification of illness is required. You cannot ask for a doctor's certificate for absences of seven days or less. The DHSS provides a self-certification form (SC1 (Rev)) which can be used for absences of between four and seven days or you can design your own. It should not be necessary to ask employees to specify their illness: signing a form to say they are ill should be enough.

## Additional sick pay

You ought to make arrangements to pay your staff more that the legal minimum when they are off work because of illness. Most voluntary organisations allow their employees a number of weeks on full pay followed by a number of weeks on half pay. If you pay your employees more than the amount of SSP due to them in a particular week, you may keep the SSP you recover from the Inland Revenue. You do not have to pay SSP in addition to normal pay.

## Pensions

The national insurance contributions you and your employees pay (see 'Paying staff', page 26) will provide them with the basic and the additional earnings related state pension when they reach retirement age. However, the state scheme is not generous. It provides no pension on earnings above the national insurance upper earnings limit, no lump sum on retirement and no benefits for the dependants of workers who die before retirement age.

In general, only the larger voluntary organisations have the resources to offer their staff the benefit of an occupational pension scheme. Most occupational pension schemes are 'contracted-out'. This means that employers and employees pay national insurance contributions at a reduced rate which entitles the workers to receive the basic state pension but not the additional pension when they retire. Instead they pay contributions to their own scheme and get a private pension when they retire.

A contracted-out pension scheme must be approved by the Occupational Pensions Board and must provide a certain standard of benefits. A contracted-out scheme involves the employer in a considerable amount of administration and depends on an open-ended commitment to the future which a small, insecurely funded voluntary group may not be able to contemplate.

It is possible, however, to join an occupational pension scheme which tops up state benefits rather than provides alternatives to them. The pension offered by such a scheme can either be directly related to the amount of money paid in or related to the employee's final salary before retirement. The first type will be more suited to a very small voluntary group. Both the employer and the individual employee can decide what they can afford to contribute to the scheme and set this as a percentage of salary. The joint contribution could be between 10 per cent and 15 per cent, with the employer and employee each paying half or some other proportion. The maximum contribution that an employee can make is 15 per cent of salary. There is no limit on the amount of the employer's contribution.

Even if you pay quite high salaries, you may not attract older and more experienced workers if you do not have some sort of occupational pension scheme. It is therefore a good idea to consider joining a suitable pension scheme. You should look carefully at the costs and benefits of a range of schemes in consultation with your staff. Pay particular attention to the issue of whether benefits are transferable when an employee leaves.

The Social Workers Pension Fund runs a number of topping up schemes particularly designed for voluntary groups and voluntary sector employers and employees are represented on the Fund's management committee.

Alternatively, it may be possible for your staff to become members of a pension scheme run by the local authority. But ensure that it does not ask for an open-ended commitment from you.

## Personnel records

However small your organisation, you are legally obliged to keep records of deductions and payments of tax, national insurance and statutory sick pay. You must also keep records of any accidents that happen to your employees (see 'Health and safety', page 22). In addition, you will need to set up a simple and efficient system of personnel records for storing essential information about your employees. The rules to follow when setting up personnel records are that you should know why you are keeping the information and you should ensure that the files are confidential. However, individual employees should be allowed access to their own files. The Data Protection Act 1984 gives employees the right to see their personnel records if these are held on a computer. However, its provisions will not be fully in force until the end of 1987 and therefore the implications of the Act are unclear. Voluntary organisations using computers are recommended to obtain a copy of the Act (see 'Further reading').

It will of course be essential to keep a record of

- the employee's name, address, home telephone number and date of birth
- name, address and telephone number of the employee's next of kin or other named person to be contacted in an emergency
- the date the employee started work
- the employee's job description
- tax code, rate of pay, hours of work, holiday entitlement
- details of any disability.

You should also keep a record of any training undertaken by the employee since starting work for you. Records of any disciplinary action taken will also be necessary. You should make arrangements for disciplinary records to be removed after an agreed time period if an employee requests it.

## Trade unions

All employees have the right to belong to a trade union and, unless there is an approved closed shop agreement, they also have the right not to belong to a trade union. In addition, employees have the right to take part in trade union activities either outside working hours or within working hours at times the employer has agreed. Industrial action does not count as a union activity.

Once some of your employees have joined a trade union, their representative may approach you asking for official recognition of the union. Recognising a union means agreeing to negotiate with it over certain terms and conditions of employment. The agreement may be wide or narrow. You may recognise a union for collective bargaining purposes and negotiate with it over the whole range of terms and conditions affecting your employees including pay. This is called a 'procedural agreement'. Or you may agree to negotiate only about disciplinary and grievance matters relating to individual union members. This is an 'individual rights agreement'. If a majority of your members belong to a trade union, it is a good idea to consider adopting a procedural agreement.

Some voluntary groups are suspicious of unions and feel good employee/employer relations in a small organisation are more likely to exist where there is no union. However, trade unions may improve relations between employers and employees by providing a forum where terms and conditions of employment can be discussed in a structured and open way. Where this happens, misunderstandings between management and staff are usually reduced. Union membership also provides support and, if necessary, protection for employees which tends to improve their morale. You can get independent advice about union recognition agreements by writing to or ringing up one of the regional offices of the Advisory, Conciliation and Arbitration Services (ACAS).

If you decide to recognise a union, an agreement will be drawn up setting out the issues to be discussed with the union, how and where these issues should be raised and what information or facilities should be provided by each side. The agreement will be signed by a management committee representative and by an officer of the union. The union should notify you of the names of its elected representatives. You should provide the union with reasonable use of office facilities, telephone, noticeboards, mailings, etc.

Officials and safety representatives elected or appointed by recognised trade unions are entitled to paid time off to carry out their duties and to undergo training. Members of recognised unions are entitled to unpaid time off to take part in union activities (see 'Time off work', page 26). You are required to disclose information to recognised trade unions which they request for collective bargaining purposes. If you have more than twenty employees, you must allow a recognised union to use your premises to hold a secret ballot for electing officers, calling or ending strikes, etc.

From November 1984, a closed shop agreement will only be approved under the law if it has been supported in a secret ballot within the last five years by either 80 per cent of the workers affected by it or by 85 per cent of those voting. Even if approved, employees are allowed not to be members if they genuinely object on grounds of conscience and in a number of other circumstances.

## Disciplinary and grievance procedures

Drawing up an agreed set of disciplinary procedures and making sure that they are followed is important for two reasons. Firstly, it promotes consistency and fairness of treatment when problems arise. Secondly, if someone is sacked and the procedures do not exist or have not been followed, you could face a claim of unfair dismissal on the grounds that the way the dismissal was handled was unfair even if the reason for the dismissal itself was fair. Agreed grievance procedures are also important to enable staff to raise matters which are affecting their ability to get on with their job. When a new project is set up, both disciplinary and grievance procedures should be fully discussed with and understood by staff before being incorporated into the written statement of terms and conditions of service.

### Disciplinary procedures
ACAS publishes a code of practice whose recommendations should be followed when drawing up procedures. It says procedures should
- be in writing
- specify to whom they apply
- provide for matters to be dealt with quickly
- indicate the disciplinary actions which may be taken
- specify the levels of management who have authority to take these actions and ensure that immediate superiors do not normally dismiss people without reference to senior management
- provide for individuals to be informed of the complaints against them and to be given an opportunity to state their case before decisions are reached
- give individuals the right to be accompanied by a trade union representative or by a fellow employee when stating their case
- ensure that except for gross misconduct (e.g. theft or assault), no employees are dismissed for a first breach of discipline
- ensure that disciplinary action is not taken until the case has been carefully investigated
- ensure that individuals are given an explanation for any penalty imposed
- provide a right of appeal and specify the procedure to be followed.

Failure to follow these guidelines will be taken into account by an industrial tribunal when deciding whether a dismissal is fair or unfair.

If there is dissatisfaction with an employee's performance or a specific complaint is made, the facts should first of all be checked. If the investigation reveals a real problem and it cannot be resolved informally by good management techniques or discussion, the agreed stages of the disciplinary procedure should be followed. These should consist of at least two oral warnings and one written warning before notice is given. At each stage, a full explanation of why disciplinary action is being taken should be made and the employee should be allowed to put her or his side of the case with the support of a union representative or friend. Specific ways in which the employee must improve should be set out and training should be offered if necessary. A date for review should be set and only if no improvement is made should matters proceed to the next stage. The employee should have the right to appeal at any stage. If notice is given, the employee should be helped to find suitable employment. Records of disciplinary procedure should be destroyed after a specified time has elapsed during which the employee's performance has been satisfactory.

In a small voluntary group, a sub-committee may need to be set up to carry out the disciplinary procedures. If so, a management committee member who is making a complaint about a member of staff should not be a member of the sub-committee considering the complaint.

## Grievance procedures

Procedures similar to those for disciplinary offences need to be agreed to enable employees to bring grievances relating to their work to the attention of other employees and management. The later stages of grievance procedures may be used for appeals against disciplinary decisions. The procedures should be designed to deal with grievances as quickly as possible.

The stages of the procedure in a small voluntary group could be the following:

- the employee raises the matter with another employee to whom she or he is responsible or with a management sub-committee
- if not resolved within five working days, the employee raises the matter with the officers of the management committee
- if not resolved within five working days, the employee raises the matter at the next management committee meeting. If a meeting is not due to be held within the next ten working days, a special meeting will be called.

An employee who is dissatisfied with the result of the grievance or disciplinary procedures is entitled to approach ACAS for advice and help.

# 4 If things go wrong

Although you may have done everything in your power to avoid it, you may still one day be faced with the prospect of dismissing staff either because of redundancy or because of their misconduct or inability to do the job. This is an unfortunate step to have to take both because the people you dismiss may face unemploynemt and because dismissals tend to have bad repercussions on other staff and on the group as a whole. They are seen as a sign of failure and can harm the organisation's reputation. You will therefore want to be sure that you have consistently followed good employment practice in selecting, managing and supporting staff and that you have done all you can to find new funding or to offer alternative jobs to redundant staff.

However, where dismissals are unavoidable, you need to be fully aware of your employees' rights not to be unfairly dismissed, their rights in relation to redundancy and the procedures to be followed when making people redundant. The following sections consider fair and unfair dismissal, redundancy and what to do if you do get taken to an industrial tribunal.

## Fair and unfair dismissal

Employment legislation allows you to dismiss an employee provided you have a valid reason for doing so and you act reasonably in the way you carry out the dismissal. For example, the employee may clearly be guilty of misconduct but if you did not follow the ACAS guidelines on disciplinary procedures before dismissing her or him, an industrial tribunal could still find the dismissal unfair.

Apart from the obvious case where you sack someone, dismissal also takes place if you do not renew a fixed term contract when it expires; if you do not allow an employee who qualifies to return to work after pregnancy to do so; or if you break the terms of your contract with the employee so that she or he resigns and claims constructive dismissal. Constructive dismissal occurs when the employer acts in such a way that the employee is justified in resigning. An example would be where the employer failed to pay the employee's salary or reduced the employee's pay without her or his agreement.

There are five types of reason which may justify dismissal. They are:

- misconduct: this is by far the most common reason for dismissal and the one that leads to the largest number of complaints of unfair dismissal
- incapability or lack of qualifications: this includes incapability due to sickness
- redundancy: although a valid reason for dismissal, an employee may have been unfairly selected for redundancy (see 'Redundancy', page 35)
- failure to fulfil a statutory requirement: for example, you may dismiss a driver who has lost her or his licence provided there is no other suitable work available
- some other substantial reason: for example, you may dismiss a temporary replacement for a woman on maternity leave when the woman returns to work, provided of course that you clearly explained that the job was temporary when you appointed the person.

Dismissing someone for one of these reasons may be judged fair provided that you acted reasonably in all the circumstances. To prove to an industrial tribunal that you acted fairly in a case of misconduct, you would have to show that you followed disciplinary practices and procedures and that the employee had due warning. In cases of incapability, you would have to prove that you provided adequate supervision and training and had given the employee time to improve. In cases of sickness incapability, you would have to show that the employment contract had been frustrated due to the employee's sickness or, in other words, that there was no hope of the employee being able to perform her or his job adequately in the foreseeable future.

In all dismissal cases, you must, if necessary, be able to show an industrial tribunal that the lines of decision making were clear and logical and all due procedures were followed to the letter. A tribunal takes into account the size and administrative resources of an organisation when deciding what is reasonable.

Dismissal is automatically unfair if it is for one of the following reasons:

- simply because of pregnancy, although the employee is still able to do her job
- because the employee is a member of a trade union or has taken part in union activities or because she or he has refused to join a trade union. Selection for redundancy on trade union grounds is also automatically unfair. Where there is an approved closed shop (see 'Trade unions', page 31), dismissal of an employee for refusing to join a union is fair unless the employee genuinely objects to membership on grounds of conscience or she or he was not a member when the closed shop was introduced and has not been one since.

Only employees who work full time (sixteen or more hours a week) and have worked for you for one year at the time of dismissal, or part time (between eight and sixteen hours a week) and have worked for you for five years, can claim unfair dismissal. Full-time employees in organisations employing twenty or fewer people and employees who started work on or after 1 June 1985 have to be employed for two years before they can make an unfair dismissal claim.

However, this qualifying period does not apply in cases of dismissal on grounds of membership or non-membership of a trade union nor in cases of dismissal on grounds of racial or sexual discrimination.

Unless dismissed for gross misconduct, employees must be given notice of dismissal and must be paid during the notice period. Gross misconduct is behaviour so bad that it justifies instant dismissal. Examples would include theft at work or assault on another member of staff. In all other cases, you must give the amount of notice you agreed when the employee's terms and conditions were decided or the legal minimum (see 'Written statement of terms and conditions of employment', page 20).

Full-time employees who have worked for you for six months or more (and part-time employees who have worked between eight and sixteen hours a week for five years) are entitled to receive a written statement of the reasons for their dismissal. If you are asked for such a statement, you must provide it within fourteen days.

If you do have to dismiss one of your employees, you ought not only to satisfy all these legal requirements but also to do what you can to help the employee find suitable alternative employment. You could, for example, give a longer notice period and allow the employee time off to look for other work. This may, of course, be inappropriate if the employee has been dismissed for gross misconduct.

## Redundancy

If all attempts to find new funding or to extend the period of a grant have failed and you have to dismiss one or more of your employees, you must be sure that you give enough notice of the forthcoming redundancies to a trade union you have recognised, that your method of selecting people for redundancy is fair, that you arrange to make redundancy payments to staff who qualify for them and that you claim a rebate from the Redundancy Pay Fund.

If you have recognised a trade union at your workplace, you must consult it about every proposed redundancy so that ways of minimising the effects of redundancy can be found. You must tell the trade union representative or district official the reasons for the redundancies, the number of staff who are to be made redundant, the method you intend to use to select people for dismissal and how the dismissals are to be carried out. This information must be put in writing. You must seriously consider and reply to any points or suggestions the union makes about the proposed redundancies.

If you are making between ten and ninety-nine people redundant over a period of thirty days or less, you must consult the union at least thirty days before the first dismissal. If 100 or more people are to go over a period of ninety days or less, you must consult the union at least ninety days before. In both these cases, you must also inform the

Department of Employment about the redundancies within the same time scale whether or not there is a recognised union to consult. To do this, get a notification form from a local jobcentre, fill it in and send it to the office marked on the form. Both these consultation processes can run concurrently with the notice period given to redundant staff.

You must ensure that you select people for redundancy in a fair and reasonable way. If you do not, you could face a claim for unfair dismissal. If funding is being withdrawn for one or more clearly defined posts, the decision will be relatively straightforward. But if you are facing a general reduction in the amount of funding available to the organisation as a whole, deciding who should be made redundant will be difficult. In this case, you must have identified the problem in good time and have decided in advance on a policy for selection for redundancy. The criteria you use for selection could be based on length of service, experience, age or ability. Whatever they are, they must be reasonable, not cause unnecessary hardship to individuals and preferably have been agreed in consultation with your staff.

It is automatically unfair to select people for redundancy on grounds of their membership or non-membership of a trade union or to select them in breach of a procedure which has previously been agreed with a trade union or staff association.

You ought to offer people threatened with redundancy another suitable job if you possibly can. If the terms and conditions of the new job are different, the employee must be given a trial period of four weeks before finally accepting the new arrangement. If retraining is needed for the new job, the trial period can be extended and a written agreement must be drawn up specifying how long it will last and any other conditions. Once the new job is accepted, the employee loses her or his right to a redundancy payment.

### Notice and time off work
You must give employees notice of redun-

dancy as for any other form of dismissal. They are entitled to the legal minimum or any longer period specified in their terms and conditions of employment.

Employees under notice of redundancy are entitled to take reasonable time off work with pay to look for other work or to arrange a training course if they work full time (sixteen hours or more a week) and have worked for you for two years, or part time (between eight and sixteen hours a week) and have worked for you for five years.

### Redundancy pay

Employees who work full time (sixteen hours or more a week) and have worked for you for two years, or part time (between eight and sixteen hours a week) and have worked for you for five years, are entitled to redundancy pay. Service before age of 18 does not count. Men and women over retirement age are not eligible.

Workers employed on fixed-term contracts of two years or over can agree in writing to forfeit their right to redundancy pay.

The amount of redundancy pay due depends on the employee's length of service, age and weekly pay. The employee gets half a week's pay for every year of service between the ages of 18 and 21; one week's pay for every year of service between the ages of 22 and 40; and one and a half week's pay for every year of service over the age of 40. The maximum number of years of service which may be counted is twenty and there is an upper limit set by government each year on the amount of weekly pay which can be counted (use the Ready Reckoner for Redundancy Payments, Form RPL2, available from the redundancy payments office).

### Making redundancy payments and getting a rebate

You are responsible for making any redundancy payments due to your employees. You must provide them with a written calculation of the amount due using form RP3, available from the redundancy payments office, which covers your area. Get the address and telephone number from a local jobcentre.

A rebate of 41 per cent of the total amount of redundancy pay can be claimed. You must claim the rebate within six months of making the redundancy payment.

You ought to set up a redundancy fund to cover payment of your 59 per cent share of redundancy pay.

### Improving on the basic minimum

Voluntary sector workers probably change jobs more frequently than other workers in order to gain further experience or promotion and forfeit in the process even the basic minimum redundancy rights described above. Yet few voluntary organisations have a redundancy agreement which gives employees any additional rights. The increasing insecurity of voluntary sector funding means both that redundancy agreements are more urgently needed and that the money to pay for any improvements is less likely to be forthcoming.

However, if the organisation's financial reserves allow it, you ought to seriously consider

* extending entitlement to redundancy pay to employees with less than two years' service
* increasing the number of weeks' redundancy pay payable
* extending the period of notice of redundancy given to employees.

### Going to a tribunal

Complaints about most of the employment rights outlined in this handbook including unfair dismissal, redundancy, equal pay, sex and race discrimination, maternity rights and trade union membership are dealt with by industrial tribunals which sit in most parts of the country. Each tribunal has a legally qualified chairman and two other members: one appointed from a trade union panel and one from an employers' panel. Industrial tribunal hearings are theoretically informal but in practice have a set procedure and many applicants are represented by lawyers. Costs are not awarded unless someone acts unreasonably or frivolously in bringing a complaint. The majority of cases dealt with by industrial tribunals are unfair dismissal claims.

If one of your employees wants to bring a case against you to an industrial tribunal, she or he will fill in a form IT1 setting out the grounds of the complaint and send it off to the Central Office of the Industrial Tribunals (COIT). You will find out about it when a copy of the employee's application is sent to you together with form IT3, also called a notice of appearance, which you are asked to fill in stating whether you intend to contest the case and if so, what your grounds are for doing so. Keep the grounds simple and factual – do not give evidence at this stage.

You should return form IT3 to the secretary of the tribunal at the address given within fourteen days of receiving it. Otherwise, you may lose your right to defend the case. You can also ask the employee to provide further and better particulars about their case.

If you feel the employee does not have a good case, you can ask the tribunal for a pre-hearing assessment. Both employer and employee are entitled to attend the assessment and comment briefly on the case. The tribunal then decides whether the case is likely to succeed. If not, the tribunal will warn either the employee or the employer that if they persist in taking the case to a full hearing, they may be liable for the costs of the other party.

## Conciliation

Except in those cases which concern redundancy pay alone, copies of all the relevant documents are sent to ACAS. A conciliation officer then approaches both employee and employer with the aim of helping them to reach a voluntary settlement. Any information given to the conciliation officer is confidential and will not be revealed at a tribunal hearing without permission. In an unfair dismissal case, the conciliation officer will try to get the employee re-instated or re-engaged on equitable terms if this is possible. If it is not, she or he will investigate whether both sides can agree on a sum of money to be awarded to

the employee as compensation. Taking part in this conciliation process is entirely voluntary and does not delay a tribunal hearing. However, if a voluntary settlement is reached with the assistance of ACAS, the employee will be asked to sign a form saying that she or he gives up the right to take the matter to a tribunal at a later date.

## Before the hearing

At any time before the tribunal hearing, you may be asked to send further information about the case to the tribunal office. You may also be asked to supply copies of relevant documents such as statements of conditions of service, notice of dismissal, records of disciplinary action, medical notes, etc. Confidential documents may be shown to the employee if the tribunal considers it is necessary. You should prepare a list of the documents you intend to take with you to the hearing to support your case and send a copy to the tribunal and to the employee. These would include age records as well as the sorts of documents mentioned above.

If you want to call witnesses to the hearing, contact them in advance. They can be ordered to attend by the tribunal if necessary. You will be given fourteen days' notice of the date of the hearing.

## The hearing

It is in your interests to attend the hearing. If you do not, the case may be decided against you in your absence. At the hearing, you or your representative will be able to explain your point of view to the tribunal, produce evidence and documents in support of your case, question your own and the employee's witnesses, respond to questions from the tribunal and sum up your case at the end. The tribunal's decision will usually be announced at the end of the hearing and a written decision with the reasons for it will be sent to you within a few weeks.

You can claim allowances for travelling and loss of earnings for yourself, your representative and any witnesses called to the hearing.

## The tribunal decision

If the tribunal finds that you have dismissed someone unfairly, it may order you to re-employ the person, although in practice this is rare, or pay a sum of money in compensation. An award of compensation is made up of two parts: a basic award of a certain number of weeks' pay for each complete year of service up to a maximum of thirty weeks' pay (this is calculated in a similar way to redundancy payments) and a compensatory award to cover loss of earnings, pensions and other expenses arising from the dismissal. The second award is at the discretion of the tribunal up to a maximum set by government each year. Special awards are given in cases of dismissal on grounds of union membership or non-membership and these can be very high.

In discrimination cases, the tribunal may make an order saying that the applicant has been unlawfully discriminated against; a recommendation that the employer should do something to remedy the situation such as offering the next similar job vacancy to the applicant; and an award of compensation.

## Reviews and appeals

It is possible in very rare circumstances to request a review of a decision made by a tribunal such as where tribunal staff made a mistake in handling the case. You must request a review within fourteen days of the decision. You may also appeal to the Employment Appeal Tribunal on a point of law and this must be done within forty-two days of the decision.

# 5 Special sorts of staff

## MSC funded posts

An increasing number of voluntary groups are setting up projects with funds provided by the Manpower Services Commission (MSC) under the Community Programme, the Voluntary Projects Programme and the Youth Training Scheme. This development represents an increase not only in the size but also in the scope of voluntary sector activity. Running training workshops and employment projects which involve activities like manufacturing, painting and decorating, repairing electrical goods and building work brings with it a host of new responsibilities, particularly in the health and safety field.

When setting up an MSC funded scheme, it is important to remember that you will become the legal employer of all the adult staff you take on and your obligations towards them are exactly the same as towards any other staff. You must be capable of taking on all the responsibilities of an employer including keeping adequate financial records and providing proper supervision for staff. If you are running a scheme under the Youth Training Scheme (YTS), you will also be responsible for the welfare and supervision of young trainees who should be treated in the same way as you would treat your employees.

The MSC issues detailed handbooks to managing agents and sponsors on all three programmes which give advice on how the project should be run particularly with regard to financial management and the presentation of accounts. The MSC does not, however, provide specific advice on employment law. You will find details of your legal duties towards your employees in the relevant sections of this handbook.

There are, however, some particular requirements to be observed in the recruitment, conditions of service and dismissal of MSC funded staff and you should also be aware of your special responsibilities towards trainees.

### Recruitment of adult staff

People recruited for jobs on the Community Programme or Voluntary Projects Programme must be unemployed. Adult staff recruited to manage and supervise YTS schemes should normally be unemployed. You should recruit people through MSC employment offices, jobcentres or the professional and executive recruitment service (PER). If you cannot find suitable applicants, you must get permission from the MSC before using alternative channels of recruitment.

You are only allowed to recruit people who are UK citizens or people who have been legally admitted into the country without employment restrictions. You cannot employ work permit holders.

Selection of staff is up to you. In the case of YTS schemes, an MSC representative may attend interviews in an advisory capacity but you choose who to appoint. The MSC also provides outline job descriptions for the posts of manager, training officer and supervisor on YTS schemes as an aid to sponsors but you are still responsible for the final form of the job descriptions used.

## Contracts

The MSC specifically advises sponsors of projects under all three programmes to avoid giving fixed term contracts to adult staff. Projects may close prematurely or the MSC may terminate them before the agreed expiry date. In either case, the MSC will not accept liability for any wages due for the remainder of the period of a fixed term contract. You should therefore issue open contracts which can be terminated by either side giving notice (see 'The contract of employment', page 16).

The MSC recommends that adult staff employed on YTS schemes, particularly those employed in a senior capacity, should serve a probationary period of up to six months. Progress during this period must be monitored closely (see 'The contract of employment').

## Conditions of service

On all three programmes, the employer is responsible for deciding rates of pay, hours of work, holiday entitlement, sick pay arrangements and disciplinary and grievance procedures. If you have other employees, you should offer MSC funded employees the same terms and conditions. If you have no other staff, you should offer the terms and conditions which apply locally to broadly similar work.

You should pay your employees the normal local rate for the job. However, the MSC sets maximum rates for reimbursing wages and these have to be taken into account if the MSC is your only source of wage income.

## Health and safety

You should be fully aware of your responsibility to provide healthy and safe working conditions for your staff (see 'Health and safety', page 21). In particular, you must identify any special risks involved in an industrial process you are supervising and know what chemicals or other substances your staff are using and how they should be handled. You can get advice from the Health and Safety Executive.

## Dismissal

Community Programme and Voluntary Projects Programme employees may only be employed for fifty-two weeks, although renewals are possible in some circumstances. They should be given notice of dismissal in accordance with the terms of their employment at the end of the period. The grounds for dismissal will normally be redundancy. The same applies to YTS staff when a scheme closes.

## Redundancy pay

Community Programme and Voluntary Projects Programme staff will not normally be entitled to redundancy pay as they will not have worked for you for two years. YTS staff are entitled to redundancy pay after two years and the MSC will reimburse the cost provided the area office has agreed to the payment in advance.

## Trainees

The MSC sets minimum standards for terms and conditions to be given to trainees on the Youth Training Scheme including holiday entitlement, sick pay, time off work, and disciplinary and grievance procedures.

In general, you ought to treat trainees as well as you would treat your other employees and ensure that they have good working conditions. Two aspects of employment practice are particularly important: insurance and health and safety.

## Insurance

Trainees are not covered by the compulsory employers' liability insurance policy that you are required to take out (see 'Insurance', page 4). You must therefore provide cover for trainees by taking out adequate public liability insurance.

You are also responsible for making sure that any sub-contractor you use is fully insured.

You should state the total amount of allowances paid to trainees in any wage declaration required by an insurer.

## Health and safety

Young people are more likely to have accidents at work than adults because they are inexperienced and possibly more prone to taking risks. It is vital, therefore, that as much as possible is done to protect the health and safety of trainees and to make them aware of dangers at work. Trainees are covered by the general provisions of the Health and Safety at Work Act 1974 rather than the specific provisions applying to employees although moves are being made to give them the full protection of employees. Your contract with the MSC also obliges you to secure the health and safety of all young people on the scheme.

If trainees are sent out on placements with other employers, you must not only make sure that these employers are fully insured, but also that they provide healthy and safe working conditions. If possible, you should visit the other employer's premises. You should also ask the employer to give full written details of health and safety procedures at the workplace and to sign a declaration that the health and safety of the trainees will be protected during the course of the placement.

Opportunities for part-time work have expanded considerably in recent years and a growing number of jobs in the voluntary sector are now part-time. However, part time employees are particularly vulnerable to overwork and it is therefore very important to draw up job descriptions that are realistic in terms of the number of hours worked. You should not expect full-time work for part time pay.

Part-time workers who work sixteen hours or more each week count as full-time workers for the purposes of all the employment rights described in this handbook which depend on hours of work and length of service. They are treated exactly the same as people working thirty-five hours a week. Employees who work between eight and sixteen hours a week are entitled to the same rights as full-time workers when they have worked for you for five years or more.

Employees who normally work sixteen hours or more a week but start to work between eight and sixteen hours a week instead are entitled to the same rights as full-time workers for the first six months of the new arrangement.

Certain rights such as protection against discrimination on grounds of race, sex or marriage, protection from victimisation or unfair dismissal for union membership or activities, and the right to equal pay do not depend on hours of work or length of service and part-time workers are automatically covered.

You should always, however, go beyond these legal minimum rights and give part-time workers the same terms and conditions of service as full-time staff but on a pro rata basis, i.e. a half-time worker should be given half the full-time rate of pay, half the holiday entitlement, and so on.

Jobsharing is a special type of part-time work which allows two employees to share one full-time job. The salary and other benefits re divided between the two employees according to the number of hours worked by each. Jobsharing has a number of

41

advantages for employers including:

- reduced staff turnover in tedious or highly stressful jobs
- greater flexibility as jobsharers can be in two places at the same time and both work at peak periods
- if one employee leaves, the other can provide some continuity until another worker is appointed
- two workers can provide a wider range of skills than one.

Employing two jobsharers rather than one worker creates no additional costs in terms of holidays, sick pay, non-statutory maternity pay or paternity pay. Only if the joint salary is above the national insurance upper earnings limit (£250 a week in April 1984) will employing two jobsharers be more expensive than employing one worker. Contributions to private pension schemes on behalf of employees will be more expensive only if the payment is a flat rate rather than a percentage of salary.

You should consider whether it is possible to open up any jobs to jobsharers and if so, advertise them as such. You will need to look carefully at how responsibilities are to be divided between the workers, how the workers will communicate with each other and whether other members of staff would be happy with the arrangement.

## Work permit holders

The only people who are allowed to work in this country without restrictions are:

- UK citizens
- Commonwealth citizens with right of abode
- People who have been granted settled status
- EEC nationals
- People who have been given leave to enter the country without employment restrictions. These are usually people who have been granted political asylum or the dependants of people who are here as workers or students.

Everyone else has to have a work permit to work here except if they are working in certain types of employment which are permit-free. These include doctors and dentists, journalists and ministers of religion.

If someone who needs a work permit applies for a job you have advertised and you want to appoint them, it will be up to you to apply for a work permit for them. Permits are only given for administrative and executive jobs or jobs which require workers who have recognised professional qualifications or who are highly qualified technicians. In addition, the overseas worker should normally be between the ages of 23 and 54 and should be able to speak English adequately.

When you apply for a work permit, you will have to show that you made adequate attempts to find suitable resident labour. You should notify the vacancy to the nearest professional and executive recruitment office or jobcentre and allow four weeks for a worker to be found. You must also advertise the job in the local or national press and send copies of the advertisements with your application for a permit giving full details of the results of the advertising. If applicants are outside the UK when they apply for the job, you must obtain work permits before they enter the country to start work. You will be responsible for paying any travelling expenses for interviews. If applicants are already in a job for which they have permits, you will still need to apply for new permits before they change jobs.

An application for a work permit should be made by filling in form OW1 which can be obtained from any jobcentre and sending it off with the required documents. You should apply at least eight weeks before you need the work permit.

## Disabled workers

If you employ twenty people or more, you are legally required to employ at least 3 per cent of registered disabled people.

The local jobcentre or employment office will contact you each year to find out whether you have been able to employ your quota of disabled workers. If no suitable disabled applicant can be found for a particular job, you can get a permit to employ a person who is not disabled. However, most employers do not fulfil the requirements of this quota scheme and the law is generally ignored.

In view of this, you ought to seek other ways of making jobs accessible to disabled people. Send details of jobs to the local disablement resettlement officer at the jobcentre or employment office and to local voluntary organisations for disabled people. There are a number of schemes which are available to help you employ disabled people. The MSC may provide special tools and equipment on free permanent loan to enable a disabled person to do a particular job. The MSC may also provide a grant to enable you to adapt your premises so that a disabled person can work there. This grant is only available when you are intending to employ a specified disabled person. In certain cases, you may be paid a grant for a number of weeks to enable you to employ a disabled person on a trial basis to see if she or he is suitable for a particular job.

# Appendix 1

## Check-list of individual employees' rights

### Discrimination

| | |
|---|---|
| Right to equal pay and conditions for like work | All employees |
| Right not to be discriminated against on grounds of race | All employees |
| Right not to be discriminated against on grounds of sex or marriage | All employees except those in organisations with five or fewer employees |
| Right not to disclose 'spent' convictions | All employees except lawyers, social workers, etc. |

### Maternity

| | |
|---|---|
| Right to be paid time off for antenatal care | All pregnant employees |
| Right to return to work after maternity leave | All full-time* employees who have worked for you for two years except those in organisations with five or fewer employees |
| Right to maternity pay | All full-time* employees who have worked for you for two years |

### Health and safety

| | |
|---|---|
| Right to paid time off work to investigate health hazards and for training in health and safety | All safety representatives appointed by a recognised trade union |

## Trade unions

| | |
|---|---|
| Right to belong to a trade union and to take part in its activities | All employees |
| Right not to belong to a trade union | All employees except where there is an approved closed shop |
| Right to paid time off for trade union duties | All full-time* employees who are officials of a recognised trade union |
| Right to time off for trade union activities | All full-time* employees who are members of a recognised trade union |

## Dismissal

| | |
|---|---|
| Right to a minimum period of notice | All full-time* employees who have worked for you for one month |
| Right to a written statement of reasons for dismissal | All full-time* employees who have worked for you for six months |
| Right not to be unfairly dismissed | Full-time* employees who have worked for you for one year if appointed before 1 June 1985; two years if appointed on or after 1 June 1985 or if you have twenty or fewer employees |
| Right not to be unfairly dismissed on grounds of union membership or activities | All employees |

## Redundancy

| | |
|---|---|
| Right to redundancy pay | All full-time* employees who have worked for you for two years |
| Right to paid time off to look for work or for a training course | All full time* employees who have worked for you for two years |

## Other

| | |
|---|---|
| Right to a written statement of terms and conditions of employment | All full-time* employees who have worked for you for thirteen weeks |
| Right to an itemised pay statement | All full-time* employees |
| Right to time off for public duties | All full-time* employees |

* Full-time employees are those working sixteen or more hours a week. Employees working between eight and sixteen hours a week are entitled to the same rights as full-time employees when they have worked for you for five years.

# Appendix 2

**Specimen statement of terms and conditions of employment†**

**Preamble**
The following statement of terms and conditions of employment is intended as a guideline only. You will need to alter and amend it to take account of your particular needs and circumstances.

**ABC Project, 200 High Road, Birmingham**
*Statement of terms and conditions of employment*
*Effective from* _____

In accordance with the provisions of the Employment Protection (Consolidation) Act 1978 as amended by the Employment Act 1980 and 1982.

This statement sets out the terms and conditions on which the ABC Project will employ you _____.
This statement also provides information on disciplinary and grievance procedures.

Your employment with the ABC Project began on _____.
Your employment with your previous employer does/does not count as part of your continuous period of employment.

Job title _____
Grade _____
Salary _____

† This specimen statement of conditions of service is based on the model statement issued by the Association of Clerical, Technical and Supervisory Staffs (ACTSS) and the statement used by the London Voluntary Service Council.

Salaries will be paid monthly in arrears on the last day of each month. Your grading and salary will be reviewed annually and any increase will be paid from 1 April. Your grading and salary will be reviewed when you receive increased responsibility. A salary increment will normally be paid annually on 1 April in addition to any cost of living award.

## Hours of work

The normal hours of work are _____am to _____pm _____to _____ . A _____hour working week is expected from all full-time staff. This does not include meal breaks.

Time off will be allowed in lieu of work done on weekday evenings and at week-ends. Such time off must be taken as soon as possible after the evening or week-end.

## Annual holidays and holiday pay

The normal annual holiday with pay is _____working days in each calendar year plus bank holidays. In exceptional cases, holiday not taken within the calendar year may be taken before 30 April of the following year. Employees joining after 1 January will be granted leave pro rata in their first leave year.

Part-time employees are entitled to holidays with pay but the total of paid holidays is to be reduced according to the ratio of hours worked to normal full-time hours.

Certain religious holidays may be granted (with or without pay or reduced pay) in certain circumstances.

## Absence due to illness and sick pay

Notification of absence from work due to illness or any other cause should be made to _____ . A self certificate is required for absences of between four and seven days. A doctor's certificate is required for absences of eight or more days.

In any consecutive twelve months an employee is allowed
- _____ sickness leave on full pay less the amount of statutory sick pay to which she or he is entitled
- a further _____ sickness leave on half pay, the employee keeping any state sickness or invalidity benefit to which she or he is entitled.

## Maternity leave and pay

A member of staff who is pregnant and who
- continues to be employed (whether or not she is at work) until eleven weeks before the expected week of confinement
- at the time has at least one year's continuous service
- informs the project in writing three weeks beforehand or as soon as is reasonably practicable therefore that she will be absent from work due to pregnancy and
- produces a medical certificate stating the expected week of confinement

is entitled to maternity pay as follows:
- six weeks on full pay less the amount of maternity benefit to which she is entitled.
- _____ weeks on half pay, the employee keeping the maternity benefit
- a final _____ weeks on half pay, the employee keeping the maternity benefit.

The project expects the pregnant member of staff who has no intention of returning to work after confinement to resign without taking advantage of this final six weeks on half pay.

Provided she complies with the conditions set out above and provided she informs the project in writing at least three weeks before her absence or as soon as reasonably practicable that she intends to return to her previous job, a member of staff will have the right to return to her previous job at any time within twenty-nine weeks of the date of confinement or to another job with the agreement of both sides. At least one week before she proposes to return to work, she must notify the project of her intention. The project may delay her return for up to four weeks on giving specified reasons in writing and she may delay it for the same period.

A member of staff is entitled to time off with full pay for attendance at antenatal clinics and this will not count against sick leave entitlement.

**Paternity leave and pay**

A member of staff who is the father or prospective father of a new-born child is entitled to up to _____ days paid paternity leave providing that he resumes work and continues to be employed by the project following the period of paternity leave and providing that the paternity leave is taken within _____ months either side of the date of birth of the child.

**Compassionate leave**

The project will give sympathetic consideration to any requests for compassionate leave on the grounds of hardship or difficulty such as bereavement, severe illness of a close relative, etc. Each request for compassionate leave will be considered on its merits without recourse to any precedent and leave may be granted with or without pay or reduced pay.

**Termination of employment**

The project will give at least four weeks' notice in writing to all members of staff and at least eight weeks' notice in writing to those who have served for over two years and less than nine years. Therefore, the project will give nine weeks' notice after nine years' service; ten weeks' notice after ten years' service; eleven weeks' notice after eleven years' service and twelve weeks' notice after twelve or more years' service.

An employee is required to give at least four weeks' notice in writing.

**Pensions**

There is no occupational pension scheme *or*

Employees are encouraged/required to join the Pension Fund. The Project and employees in the Fund are both required to contribute to the Social Workers Pension Fund at current rates.

**Trade union**

You may join the trade union of your choice *or*

You are encouraged to become a member of an appropriate trade union *or*

The ABC Project has recognised that _____

is the representative body for staff for certain purposes. You will be supplied with a copy of the recognition agreement. You are recommended to join _____ if you wish to do so.

**Time off for public duties**

The Project will permit time off to be taken for public duties as set out in the Employment Protection Act 1978 and in addition as is considered reasonable by the Project.

Payment for time off work for public duties will be made at the discretion of the Project. Employees are required to claim attendance allowances and expenses and to remit them to the Project, excluding travelling and subsistence costs, to set against salary costs.

**Subsistence and travelling expenses**

Subsistence and travelling expenses are paid when employees are away from the office on duty. The current scale of allowances is available on request.

**Disciplinary procedure**

The following four stages will apply to unsatisfactory work and conduct:

*Stage 1: oral warning*

A disciplinary sub-committee composed of members of the management committee explains to the employee the reasons for taking disciplinary action and discusses plans for overcoming the problem. The discussion and plans are recorded and a reasonable time for review is agreed.

### Stage 2: oral warning
If the sub-committee considers at the time of the review that progress is unsatisfactory, there will be a further discussion and re-examination of the plans for improvement with the employee. This discussion and the revised plans will again be recorded and a further reasonable time for review will be agreed with the employee.

### Stage 3: written warning
If progress is still unsatisfactory at the time of the review, there will be a further discussion with the employee. This discussion and the plans for improvement will be recorded and a copy will be given to the employee clearly stating that lack of improvement by the date set for review will result in dismissal.

### Stage 4: final written warning and dismissal
Should progress not be made by the time of the review, the employee should be given a written statement of why dismissal is taking place. Notice will be given and assistance will be offered to enable the employee to find more suitable alternative employment.

At all of these stages, the employee may be represented by a trade union official or other work colleague.

Written records of disciplinary discussions will be shown to the employee before being filed.

An employee's request to have written warnings removed from the records will be agreed to when a suitable time period has elapsed.

### Appeals
If an employee wishes to appeal against any disciplinary decision, the following stages shall be followed:

### Stage 1
The employee raises the matter with the officers of the management committee. If it is not resolved within five working days, it should be referred to stage 2.

### Stage 2
The employee raises the matter at the next available meeting of the management committee. If no meeting is due to be held within ten working days, a special meeting will be called.

At both these stages, the employee may be represented by a trade union official or other work colleague.

If the employee is not satisfied with the outcome, she or he can approach the Advisory, Conciliation and Arbitration Service for advice or appeal to an industrial tribunal.

### Grievance procedure
An employee who has a grievance about employment should follow the procedure outlined below.

### Stage 1
The employee raises the matter with _____

### Stage 2
If not resolved within five working days, the employee raises the matter with the officers of the management committee.

### Stage 3
If not resolved within five working days, the employee raises the matter at the next management committee meeting. If a meeting is not due to be held within ten working days, a special meeting will be called.

At all of these stages, the employee may be represented by a trade union official or other work colleague.

If the employee is not satisfied with the outcome, she or he can approach the Advisory, Conciliation and Arbitration Service for advice or appeal to an industrial tribunal.

Signed on behalf of the ABC Project _____

Date _____

# Useful addresses

Advisory, Conciliation and Arbitration
Services (ACAS)
11–12 St James Square
London SW1Y 4LA
01-214 6000

Association of Clerical, Technical and
Supervisory Staffs (ACTSS)
Transport House
Smith Square
London SW1P 3JB
01-828 7788

Association of Scientific, Technical and
Managerial Staffs (ASTMS)
10 Jamestown Road
London NW1 9ES
01-267 4422

British Institute of Management
Management House
Parker Street
London WC2B 5PT
01-405 3456

Central Office of Industrial Tribunals
93 Ebury Bridge Road
London SW1W 8RE
01-730 9161

Commission for Racial Equality
Elliot House
10–12 Allington Street
London SW1E 5EH
01-828 7022

Department of Employment
Caxton House
Tothill Street
London SW1H 9NF
01-213 3000

Department of Employment
Overseas Labour Section
Caxton House
Tothill Street
London SW1H 9NF
01-213 3332

Department of Health and Social Security
Alexander Fleming House
Elephant and Castle
London SE1 6BY
01-407 5522

Equal Opportunities Commission
Overseas House
Quay Street
Manchester M3 3HN
061-833 9244

*Health and Safety Executive*
Baynards House
1 Chepstow Place
London W2 4TF
01-229 3456

*Home Office*
50 Queen Anne's Gate
London SW1H 9AT
01-213 3000

*Home Office*
Immigration and Nationality Service
Lunar House
Wellesley Road
Croydon
Surrey CR9 2BY
01-686 0333

*Income Data Services*
140 Great Portland Street
London W1N 5TA
01-580 0521

*Industrial Society*
3 Carlton House Terrace
London SW1Y 5DG
01-839 4300

*Inland Revenue*
Somerset House
New Wing
Strand
London WC2R 1LB
01-438 6622

*Institute of Personnel Management*
IPM House
Camp Road
London SW19 4UW
01-946 9100

*Labour Research Department*
78 Blackfriars Road
London SE1 8HF
01-928 3649

*Local Authorities Conditions of Service Advisory Board (LACSAB)*
41 Belgrave Square
London SW1X 8NZ
01-235 6081

*Manpower Services Commission*
Moorfoot
Sheffield S1 4PQ
0742-753275

*National and Local Governent Officers Association (NALGO)*
1 Mabledon Place
London WC1H 9AX
01-388 2366

*National Council for Voluntary Organisations*
26 Bedford Square
London WC1B 3HU
01-636 4066

*New Ways to Work*
347A Upper Street
London N1 0PD
01-226 4026

# Further reading

An asterisk indicates publications that are free.

**Choosing a salary scale**

Department of Education and Science. *Scales of Salaries for Teachers in Further Education in England and Wales*, HMSO, 1983.

Local Authorities Conditions of Service Advisory Board. *Conditions of Service for Further Education Teachers*, LACSAB, 1982.

Local Authorities Conditions of Service Advisory Board. *The National Joint Council Scheme of Conditions of Service (the Purple Book)*, LACSAB, 8th edn, 1975.

Local Authorities Conditions of Service Advisory Board. *Report of the Joint Negotiating Committee for Youth Workers and Community Centre Wardens*, LACSAB, 1983.

**Discrimination**

Equal Opportunities Commission. *Equality at Work: a guide to the employment provisions of the Sex Discrimination Act 1975,*\* EOC, 1982.

Equal Opportunities Commission. *The Sex Discrimination Act and Advertising: guidance notes,*\* EOC, 1980.

Home Office. *Racial Discrimination: a guide to the Race Relations Act 1976,*\* Home Office, 1977.

Home Office. *Sex Discrimination: a guide to the Sex Discrimination Act 1975,*\* Home Office, 1975.

**Insurance**

Pedlar, P. *Insurance Protection: a guide for voluntary organisations and voluntary workers*, National Council for Voluntary Organisations, 1983.

## The contract of employment

Incomes Data Services. *Employment Contracts* (IDS Handbook series, no. 21), IDS, 1981.

## Written statement of terms and conditions of employment

Department of Employment. *Written Statement of Main Terms and Conditions of Employment*\* (Employment legislation: 1), DE, 1983.

## Health and safety

Craig, M. *Office Workers' Survival Handbook: a guide to fighting health hazards in the office,* British Society for Social Responsibility in Science, 1981.

Earscott, P. *An Employer's Guide to Health and Safety Management,* Kogan Page, revised edn, 1980.

Health and Safety Commission. *Guidance Notes on Employers' Policy Statement for Health and Safety at Work*\* (Leaflet HSC 6), HSC.

Health and Safety Commission. *Health and Safety: safety representatives and safety committees,* HMSO, 1977.

Health and Safety Commission. *Health and Safety at Work Act 1974: advice to employers*\* (Leaflet HSC 3), HSC.

Kinnersley, P. *The Hazards of Work and How to Fight Them,* Pluto Press, 1974.

## Maternity Rights

Cousins, J. *Maternity Rights for Working Women*, National Council for Civil Liberties, 1983.

Department of Employment, *Employment Rights for the Expectant Mother*\* (Employment legislation: 4), DE, 1982.

Incomes Data Services. *Maternity Rights*\* (IDS Handbook series, no. 26), IDS, 1983.

## Equal Opportunities

Commission for Racial Equality. *Code of Practice for the Elimination of Racial Discrimination and the Promotion of Equality of Opportunity in Employment,*\* CRE, 1983.

Equal Opportunities Commission. *Code of Practice for the Elimination of Sex and Marriage Discrimination and the Promotion of Equality of Opportunity in Employment*, EOC, 1985.

Equal Opportunities Commission. *A Model Equal Opportunity Policy,*\* EOC, 1983.

## Time off work

Advisory, Conciliation and Arbitration Service. *Time Off for Trade Union Duties and Activities*\* (Code of Practice – 3), ACAS.

Department of Employment. *Facing Redundancy: time off for job hunting or to arrange training*\* (Employment legislation: 6), DE, 1982.

Department of Employment. *Time Off for Public Duties*\* (Employment legislation: 12), DE, 1982.

Health and Safety Commission. *Health and Safety at Work: safety representatives and safety committees,* HMSO, 1977.

Health and Safety Commission. *Time Off for the Training of Safety Representatives*\* (Leaflet HSC 9), HSC.

## Paying staff: PAYE and national insurance

Department of Employment. *Itemised Pay Statement*\* (Employment legislation: 8), DE, 1982.

Department of Health and Social Security. *Employer's Guide to National Insurance Contributions*\* (Leaflet NP15), DHSS.

Department of Health and Social Security. *National Insurance Contribution Rates and Statutory Sick Pay Rates*\* (Leaflet NI208), DHSS.

Inland Revenue. *Employer's Guide to PAYE*\* (Booklet P7), IR.

## Sick pay
Department of Health and Social Security. *Employer's Guide to Statutory Sick Pay*\* (Leaflet NI227), DHSS.

Department of Health and Social Security. *National Insurance Contribution Rates and Statutory Sick Pay Rates*\* (Leaflet NI208), DHSS.

Labour Research Department. *Statutory Sick Pay*, LRD Publications Ltd, 1983.

## Pensions
Department of Health and Social Security. *Employer's Guide to Occupational Pension Schemes and Contracting-out*\* (Leaflet NP23, DHSS.

Department of Health and Social Security. *Your Retirement Pension*\* (Leaflet NP32), DHSS.

## Personnel records
Data Protection Act 1984, Her Majesty's Stationery Office, 1984.

Data Protection Registrar. *An Introduction and Guide to the [Data Protection] Act*, Data Protection Registrar, 1985

Elbra, R.A. *Guide to the Data Protection Act*, NCC Publications, 1984.

National Computing Centre. *Guide to the Data Protection Act*, NCC, 1984.

## Trade Unions
Advisory, Conciliation and Arbitration Service. *Disclosure of Information to Trade Unions for Collective Bargaining Purposes*\* (Code of Practice – 2), ACAS, 1977.

Advisory, Conciliation and Arbitration Service. *Time Off for Trade Union Duties and Activities*\* (Code of Practice – 3), ACAS, 1977.

Department of Employment. *Closed Shop Agreements and Arrangements – Code of Practice,*\* DE, 1983.

Department of Employment. *Union Membership Rights and the Closed Shop*\* (Employment legislation: 7), DE, 1983.

Department of Employment. *Union Secret Ballots*\* (Employment legislation: 15), DE, 1982.

Incomes Data Services. *Employing Union Members* (IDS Handbook series, no. 18), IDS, 1981.

Incomes Data Services. *Right to be Recognised* (IDS Handbook series, no. 18), IDS, 1981.

## Disciplinary and grievance procedures
Advisory, Conciliation and Arbitration Service. *Disciplinary Practice and Procedures in Employment*\* (Code of Practice – 1), ACAS, 1977.

## Fair and unfair dismissal
Department of Employment. *Fair and Unfair Dismissal: a guide for employers,*\* DE, 1982.

Department of Employment. *Rights on Termination of Employment*\* (Employment legislation: 14), DE, 1983.

Department of Employment. *Unfairly Dismissed?*\* (Employment legislation: 13), DE, 1983.

Henderson, J. *The Law on Unfair Dismissal: guidance for small firms,*\* DE, 1982.

Incomes Data Services. *Handling Dismissals* (IDS Handbook series: no. 25), IDS, 1983.

Incomes Data Services. *Unfair Dismissal* (IDS Handbook series: no. 25), IDS, 1983.

## Redundancy

Department of Employment. *Facing Redundancy? Time Off for Job Hunting or to Arrange Training* (Employment legislation: 6), DE, 1982.

Department of Employment. *Procedure for Handling Redundancies* (Employment legislation: 2), DE, 1985.

Department of Employment. *Redundancy Payments* (Employment legislation: 16), DE, 1984.

Department of Employment. *Rules Governing Continuous Employment and a Week's Pay* (Employment legislation: 11), DE, 1983.

Incomes Data Services. *Redundancy* (IDS Handbook series: no. 24), IDS, 1982.

## Going to a tribunal

Advisory, Conciliation and Arbitration Service. *Conciliation in Complaints by Individuals to Industrial Tribunals: the ACAS role,* ACAS, 1979.

Department of Employment. *Industrial Tribunals Procedure,* DE, 1983.

Incomes Data Services. *Going to a Tribunal* (IDS Handbook series: no. 16), IDS, 1980.

## MSC funded posts

Labour Research Department. *Youth Training: a negotiator's guide,* LRD Publications Ltd, 1983.

Manpower Services Commission. *Community Programme: the agents' and sponsors' handbook,* MSC, 1981.

Manpower Services Commission. *Health and Safety on the Youth Training Scheme: guidance for providers of training, education and work experience,* MSC, 1982.

Manpower Services Commission. *Youth Training Scheme: community projects sponsors' handbook,* MSC.

Manpower Services Commission. *Youth Training Scheme: a handbook for managing agents,* MSC.

Manpower Services Commission. *Youth Training Scheme: sponsors' handbook for training workshops,* MSC.

Manpower Services Commission. *Voluntary Projects Programme: sponsors' handbook,* MSC.

## Part-time workers and jobsharers

Equal Opportunities Commission. *Job Sharing: improving the quality and availability of part-time work,* EOC, 1981.

Hopwood, S. & Baxter, M. *Job Sharing and Voluntary Organisations,* New Ways to Work and National Council for Voluntary Organisations, 1983.

New Ways to Work. *Job Sharing: a guide for employers,* New Ways to Work, 1981.

Sedley, A. *Part-time Workers Need Full-time Rights,* National Council for Civil Liberties, 1980.

## Work permit holders

Gray, S. & Lowe, A. *The Ins and Outs of Immigration and Nationality Law,* National Association of Citizens Advice Bureaux, 1983.

## Disabled workers

Kettle, M. & Massie, B. *The Employers' Guide to Disabilities,* Royal Association for Disability and Rehabilitation, 1982.

## General

Chandler, P. *An A-Z of Employment and Safety Law,* Kogan Page, 1981.

Hepple, B. & O'Higgins, P. *Employment Law*, Sweet and Maxwell, 1981.

Lewis, D. *Essentials of Employment Law*, Institute of Personnel Management, 1983.

McMullen, J. *Rights at Work,* Pluto Press, 2nd edn, 1983.

Newell, D. *The New Employment Law Legislation: a guide to the Employment Acts 1980 and 1982,* Kogan Page, 1983.

Selwyn, N. *Law of Employment,* Butterworth, 1980.

Slade, E. *Employment Handbook,* Tolley, 3rd edn, 1983.